365
Things
to Make
and Do Right Now!

Crafts by Susan Hunter-Jones and Katy Rhodes
Photography by Darren Sawyer
Written by Kirsty Neale, Susan Hunter-Jones, and Katy Rhodes
Step art by Dynamo Limited
Spot art by Caroline Martin
Edited by Laura Baker
Designed by Sally Garner and Clare Phillips
Production by Jonathan Wakeham

First published by Parragon in 2012

Parragon
Queen Street House
4 Queen Street
Bath BA1 1HE, UK
www.parragon.com

ISBN 978-1-4454-8796-0
Printed in China

365 Things to Make and Do Right Now!

PaRragon

Bath · New York · Singapore · Hong Kong · Cologne · Delhi
Melbourne · Amsterdam · Johannesburg · Shenzhen

Contents

Welcome to

365 Things to Make and Do RIGHT NOW!

This book is filled with 365 cool things you can make RIGHT NOW! Whether you feel like painting, drawing, sticking, cutting, stitching, stamping, or ripping, there's plenty to keep you busy.

The projects all have simple instructions to follow and helpful photos. Some even have extra ideas for the craft! It's good to remember that your project doesn't have to look exactly the same as the one in the picture. The instructions are there to guide you, but you can use your own creativity, too!

How to use this book

With 365 projects to choose from (and an extra one for a leap year!), you could try making one project every day for a whole year. Or, dip into the book when you're feeling crafty, maybe on weekends or during school vacations ...
There's no right or wrong way to make!

What will I need?

Nearly all the materials you'll need are things you can find around the house. You might want to start collecting some of them now so they'll be ready and waiting the next time you're feeling arty. Find a big box and use it to stash supplies—save up yogurt pots, keep leftover wrapping paper, ask your parents if you can have old newspapers, and don't throw away the stick next time you eat ice cream on a stick!

Look for...

You will need:

Some pages start with a list of supplies. Read through it carefully before you get started. If you don't have everything on the list, see if there's something else you can use, or come back to the project another day. There are plenty of others you can do RIGHT NOW instead!

▼! Ask an adult for help with this craft.

When you see this, grab yourself a grown-up! It means there's a tricky part coming up. You'll need an adult to help or to watch and make sure you stay safe.

TiP!

You'll find these handy hints throughout the book. They give suggestions for making things easier or give you extra ideas for projects.

What next?

Read through the next few pages. You'll find a list of materials that could come in handy and some useful techniques. Come back to these at any time—maybe before you start a new project or if you need some extra help along the way. Then ...

Ready, set, MAKE!

Materials

Around the house

Save things from around the house to be ready to make—things from the kitchen, the yard, the bathroom, and even your bedroom. Remember to ask permission before you take anything, especially if you're going to paint it, glue it, or cut it up!

Cardboard and cardstock

Colored paper

Paper towel

Kitchen sponges

Paper plates, bowls, cups

Plastic cups

String

Curly ribbon

Yarn

Aluminum foil

Foil trays or pans

Paper cupcake liners

Cotton buds

Straws

Cotton balls

Cotton batting

Tissue paper

Dried food (lentils, beans, etc.)

Seeds, stones, sand, pinecones, leaves, twigs from the yard

Garden stakes

Wooden spoons

Rubber bands

Brown paper

Brass fasteners

Bubble wrap

TIP!
Recycle cardboard from packaging, cereal boxes, or stiff manila envelopes.

Handy extras

You might already have some of these supplies at home, but if not, they're all things you can find in craft stores, and they don't need to cost very much. It's useful to have some of them ready and waiting when you want to get started on a project!

Ribbon
Felt
Sequins
Gold/silver pens
Glitter
Craft feathers
Buttons
Beads

TIP!

Cover clothes and work surfaces before you make your crafts, in case anything gets messy!

Crafty tools

Pack these into your craft tool kit and you'll be all set to make just about anything!

Scissors
White glue
Glue stick
Ruler
Pencil
Markers
Colored pencils
Crayons

Tape
Double-sided tape
Masking tape
Paintbrushes
Glue spreaders
Craft paints
Fabric paint

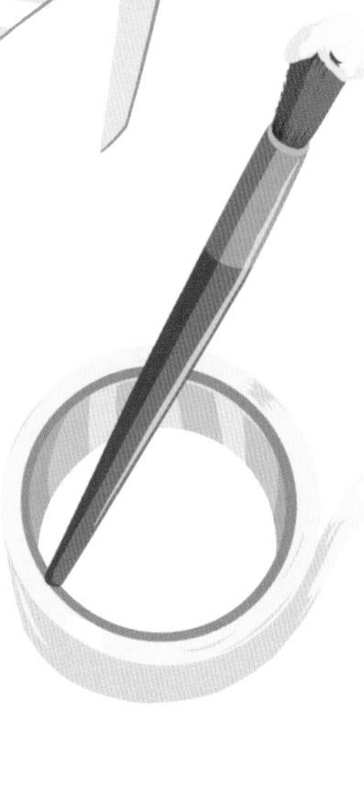

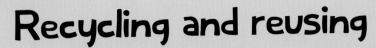

Recycling and reusing

The things on this page are mostly old, used, or unwanted. Some of them might already be on their way to the trash or the recycling bin, but you can save them for crafts! Turning trash into something new is tons of fun—it's good for the planet and, best of all, it's free!

Wrapping-paper scraps

Fabric scraps

Candy wrappers

Buttons

Shells

Beads

Cardboard packaging

Old T-shirts

Old sweaters

Socks

Tights

Gloves/mittens

Ice cream sticks

Newspaper

Magazines

Plastic bags

Bottle-tops

Yogurt cups (cleaned out!)

Plastic bottles (large water bottles, small milk bottles)

Cardboard paper-towel rolls

Egg cartons

Glass jars

Old rubber boots

Mesh bag from onions

Old jigsaw-puzzle pieces

Tip!

Don't recycle or reuse anything without checking with an adult first.

Techniques

Sticky stuff
Different projects need different types of stick!

White glue is runny. It's stronger than a glue stick, but it can make thin paper wrinkly. You can add it to paper, cardstock, or fabric with a brush. It dries quite quickly and is good for gluing cardstock and heavy materials.

A glue stick is solid and dries very quickly. It's good to use on paper projects.

Double-sided tape comes on a roll, like normal tape, but one side is covered with shiny paper. To use it, tear or cut off a piece and press it onto your project. Then peel off the paper backing to show the second sticky side. It's quite strong and is useful for joining pieces of paper and cardboard together without having to wait for glue to dry.

Handy patterns

Patterns are really useful tracing tools for cutting out exact shapes. They can be simple shapes, like circles and stars, or more complicated designs. Lots of the projects in this book use patterns.

You can make most of the easy shapes on your own. Draw them onto cardstock and then cut them out, ready to trace.

For a symmetrical shape, such as a heart, fold the cardstock in half first. Draw half the shape against the fold and cut it out. When you unfold and flatten the cardstock again, your pattern will be perfectly neat and symmetrical!

Tip!

Don't throw patterns away when you've finished a project. You might want to use them again! Find an envelope roughly the same size as this book, and fix it to the last page with a paper clip. Slip all your patterns inside.

What to use

It's best to make patterns from thin cardstock. This makes them easy to cut out but strong enough to trace around.

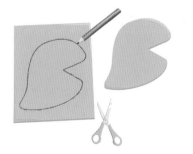 

What to do

To use your patterns, place them on the back of your paper or fabric. Trace around the edges with a pen or pencil to make an exact copy of the shape. Then cut out!

From the page

To copy shapes you like in this book, grab some tracing paper (or wax paper from the kitchen) and place over the page. Trace the shape in pencil. Remove from the book, then scribble heavily on the back of the paper, filling in the shape. With the scribbled side face down on a piece of cardstock, draw back over the traced shape. Take the paper away to reveal the outline on your cardstock, ready for you to cut out as your pattern.

Sewing skills

Sometimes it seems quicker to glue things together, but sewing can make your projects stronger, neater, and more stylish! Try learning these few basic stitches.

Starting and finishing

Before you start sewing, tie a knot in the end of your thread. When you've finished, tie another knot or go back over the last stitch a few times. Trim the ends close to the knot, but not so close that it's easily undone.

Buttons

To sew on a button, hold it in place and push the needle up through the fabric and one of the button holes. Take it back down through the opposite hole and the fabric underneath. Repeat this a few more times, until the button feels secure.

Tip!

If your button has four holes, sew through the other two in the same way!

Thread

Thread can be made of one thin strand, or you can double up for something thicker and stronger. Stitches made with thin thread are harder to see than stitches made with thick thread, which can be useful when sewing pieces together. Just remember that sometimes you'll want to use thick thread or even embroidery thread to decorate!

Running stitch

1 Thread your needle and tie a knot at the end. Bring the needle up through the fabric. Pull firmly so the knot is against the back of the fabric.

2 Push the needle back down about a quarter inch away. Pull the thread all the way through. That's your first stitch!

3 Keep going, moving the needle in and out of the fabric to make more stitches about a quarter inch apart. Tie a knot under the fabric at the end when you're done and trim.

Whip stitch

1 Thread your needle and tie a knot at the end. Push the needle through your fabric, from back to front, roughly a quarter inch from the edge, pulling firmly so the knot is against the back of the fabric.

2 Do the same again, pushing the needle up from back to front about a quarter inch away. The thread will loop over the edges of the material.

3 Keep going, making more stitches in the same way. Don't pull the thread too tightly, or your material will look twisted and crooked! Tie a knot under the fabric at the end when you're done and trim.

14

Home Sweet Home

Curly coils

Make a cool, colorful frame for your favorite picture!

You will need:

- Picture or photo
- Sharp pencil
- Colored paper
- White glue
- Cardboard
- Ruler
- Scissors
- Tape

⚠ Ask an adult for help with this craft.

1

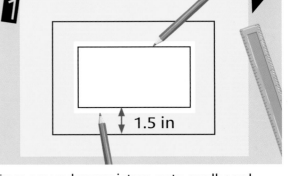

1.5 in

Trace around your picture onto cardboard, then draw a rectangle slightly smaller than the picture. Measure a 1.5 in border around the outside. Cut along this line. To cut out the center, make a hole with a sharp pencil, put your scissors in, and cut up to the outline.

2

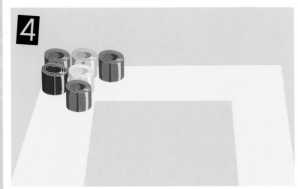

Make coils by rolling a piece of paper around a pencil. Slide the paper off and push it backward and forward on the table to make the roll even tighter.

3

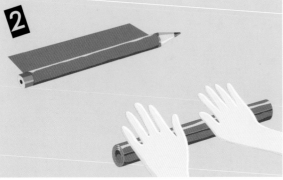

Cut the paper roll into short pieces. Squash each one into a nice, round shape with your fingers.

4

Dip each coil into glue and press down onto the cardboard frame. Use coils made from different paper colors and mix them up to make a bright pattern. Stick your picture to the back of the frame with tape.

Did you know?
Making pictures or decorations from strips of rolled-up paper is known as quilling.

Flower power
The flowers on this round frame have six coiled petals. Place each one on the frame to see how many will fit before you start gluing them down.

TiP!
To make a coil bigger, gently pull it apart and re-roll the paper less tightly.

Bugs and butterflies
Make butterfly antennae by unrolling one end of a paper coil.

17

Picture perfect

Recycle a plain wooden picture frame, or try cutting your own from cardboard. Give it a fancy new look with these fun decorating ideas.

Back to nature

Place flowers and leaves between sheets of white paper, then flatten under a pile of heavy books for two weeks. When they're flat and dry, glue to your frame. Add clear tape on top to protect the petals.

Or try breaking sticks into pieces, and arrange them on the frame with pinecones. Stick into place with dabs of white glue.

Button up

Cover your frame in a lot of buttons. Choose a mixture of colors or pick one favorite. Use different sizes and set them in place with white glue.

Puzzle pizzazz

Paint the outside pieces from an old jigsaw puzzle in different colors. Join them together, then glue to a cardboard frame. For extra sparkle, cover with white glue and sprinkle glitter on top.

Paper mosaic

Make a mosaic pattern by gluing small squares of paper to a piece of cardstock. Let dry, then cut out a heart-shaped frame. Glue a loop of ribbon to the back so you can hang up your finished frame.

⚠ Ask an adult for help with this craft.

Twisted tissue

Cut tissue paper into small squares. Fold each square around the end of a pencil, dip into glue, and press onto the frame. Stick them as close together as you can for a colorful, textured effect.

Seeds and grains

Stick thin strips of corrugated cardboard sideways along each edge of your frame to make a border. Spread glue over the front of the frame, then sprinkle seeds and grains on top. Glue a ribbon around the outside edge of the frame, leaving a loop for hanging at the top.

Funky bags

Stash your stuff in one of these chic drawstring bags!

You will need:

- Fabric
- Scissors
- Ribbon
- Large bead
- Ruler or tape measure
- Pencil
- White glue
- Glue spreader

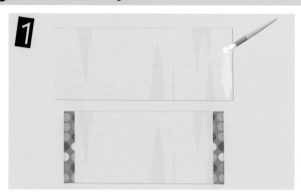

1 Measure and cut out a 12 x 6 inch piece of fabric. With the wrong side facing you, use your glue spreader to brush glue along the short edges. Fold over half an inch at each end and press down. Allow to dry.

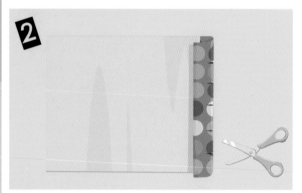

2 Fold one glued edge over on itself and cut small slits into the fabric. Do the same at the other end.

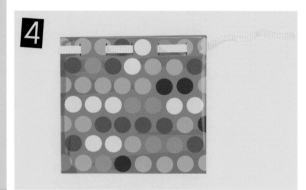

3 With the right side facing you, brush glue halfway down each long edge. Fold in half and line up the top edges exactly. Press firmly along the sides and allow to dry. The bag will now be inside out.

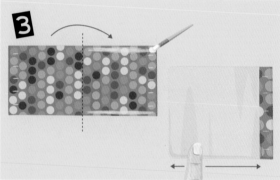

4 Turn your bag right side out, so that the pattern is on the outside. Cut a piece of ribbon 20 inches long and thread in and out of the snipped holes around the top of the bag.

5 Push the ribbon ends through a large bead, then tie them together. To close your bag, pull the ribbon so it gathers up the material. Slide the bead in place to hold the bag shut.

Tip!

Which side of fabric is which?

The **right side** is brighter and more colorful, especially if the fabric has a pattern.

The **wrong side** is more faded, and it's usually hidden on the inside of a project done with fabric.

Button bling

Thread string through the holes in your bag and finish off with a button, instead of using ribbon and a bead.

Tip!

To make a longer handle, use a longer piece of ribbon or string. Nice and easy!

21

Window dazzlers

Save up some shiny candy wrappers and use them to make your own stained-glass windows.

You will need:

- Thin cardstock
- Pencil
- Colored candy wrappers
- Round and/or flower-shaped sequins
- Thick paper
- Clear tape
- White glue
- Ribbon
- Scissors

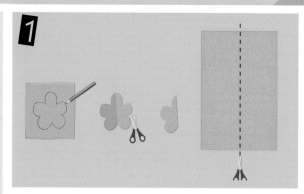

1 Draw a 5-petal flower, roughly 3 inches tall, onto a piece of thin cardstock. Cut it out, then cut it in half. Cut a 4 x 11-inch strip of thick paper.

2 Fold the paper in half lengthwise. Place the flower pattern on the fold and trace around it three times, spacing the shapes evenly. Cut out all three flowers. Round off the corners of the paper.

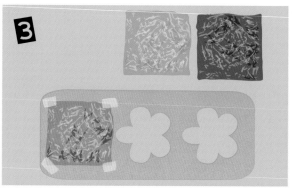

3 Unfold the paper and smooth it flat. Place a candy wrapper behind each flower-shaped hole and tape it to the back of the paper.

4 Turn the paper over and glue sequins to the front using small dots of glue.

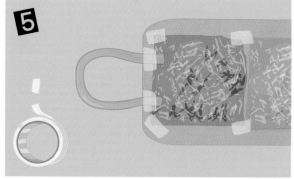

5 When the glue is dry, cut a length of ribbon to make a hanger for your decoration. Tape the ends neatly in place on the back of the paper.

Super stars

Make a star-shaped pattern instead of a flower and finish off your decoration with starry sequins or stickers.

Ssssnake!

Draw and cut out a snake from your paper strip. Tape strips of candy wrappers across the hole, mixing up the colors for a striped effect. Add sequins for eyes and use an extra piece of candy wrapper to make a forked snake's tongue.

! Ask an adult for help with this craft.

Spooky mobiles

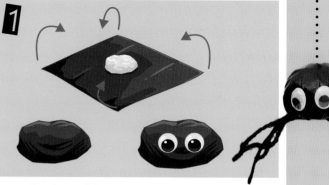

1 To make the spider, roll some aluminum foil into a ball, then flatten it a little bit. Cut out a piece of black plastic and wrap it around the foil. Tape it underneath to hold in place. Glue on some googly eyes.

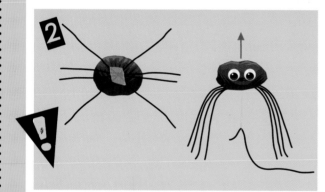

2 For the legs, cut four pieces of black yarn. Tape them under the spider's body. Thread an extra piece of yarn up through the body to make a loop for hanging. Tie a knot at the bottom and tie a loop at the top.

3 Roll a bigger ball of foil to make a bat. Cut a wide piece of plastic and place the foil in the middle. Wrap the plastic around the foil and tape down. Gather the extra plastic on each side and tie with yarn to make wings.

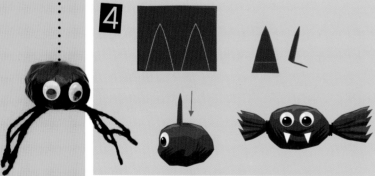

4 Draw two bat ears onto black cardstock. Cut out. Fold the straight ends back. Glue to the top of the head. Glue on two googly eyes. Cut out small triangles of white cardstock for fangs. Add a yarn hanger, as before.

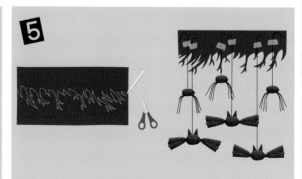

5 Make a few more bats and some extra spiders. Cut out a strip of black cardstock and draw spooky twig shapes along the bottom edge. Cut them out. Tape bats and spiders to the back using the yarn hangers.

Tip!

Hang the bats and spiders at different heights along your cardboard strip. They'll have more space to move around and will also make for a bigger, spookier display!

Tip!

When you glue the bat ears into place, make sure the folded tab sections face toward the back.

Going for ghouls!

Roll a ball of foil and stick some double-sided tape around the widest part. Cut out a circle of plastic, with wavy or spiky edges. Place the ball of foil in the middle of the circle. Gather the plastic around the foil, pressing it onto the tape to hold in place. Glue on two black circles for eyes and add a yarn hanger, as before.

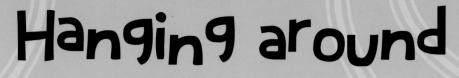

Hanging around

Add some style to your room with these dazzling dangling decorations!

Spiral spinner

Starting in the middle, draw a spiral onto a circle of cardstock. Cut along the line, then glue a loop of thread in the center.

Beads in a spin

Make a spiral spinner, as before. Take some beads and tie each one to a short piece of thread. Tape the thread ends to the bottom of the spiral, so the beads dangle from the finished spinner.

Wavy buttons

Use wavy-edged scissors to cut out your spiral, or draw a wavy line and cut with normal scissors. Glue buttons along the spinner to make it more colorful.

TIP!
Tie tiny bells to the threads instead of beads for a fun, jingly decoration!

TIP!
Shiny or glittery cardstock will catch the light as your spinner twirls for an even cooler effect.

The dreamcatcher

Cut a long strip of thick paper and punch holes all the way along. Glue the ends together to make a ring. Thread in and out of the holes, going across the ring. Add beads to the thread as you go. Make a loop at the top for hanging, and glue or tie on some feathers at the bottom.

On a plate

To make a different kind of dreamcatcher, cut the middle out of a paper plate. Paint the rim and make holes around the inside edge. Add thread and beads, as before. Finish off with feathers and a loop for hanging.

It's a sign

1

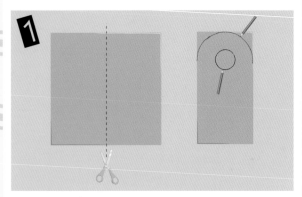

Cut a piece of cardstock to roughly 4 x 8 inches. Trace around a small bowl to make a curve at the top. Draw around an egg cup to mark out a hole in the middle.

2

Cut around the curve at the top. Use a sharp pencil to make a hole in the center of the circle. Push your scissors through to cut out the circle. Snip half-inch slots in from the circle.

3

Cut out extra pieces of cardstock to make arms and legs. Glue them into place. Cut out circles to make lights and eyes, and more rectangles for the mouth, teeth, chest, and feet. Glue them on to finish off your robot.

TiP!

The slots around the hole are there to make sure that your sign will fit around all kinds of doorknobs. You can also adjust the size of the hole if necessary.

TiP!

Add some scraps of aluminum foil or use silver paper to give your 'bot a cool, metallic look.

Twinkle, twinkle

Start by cutting out a piece of cardstock, just like before, but this time add a curve shape at the bottom, too. Draw a moon and some stars onto some paper, using markers. Cut out each shape and glue to the sign. Doodle on silver stars and swirls to add some extra sparkle.

29

Animal crackers

Create a crazy chain of hanging animals by linking up their arms, legs, bodies, trunks, or tails!

Dot frogs

The more arms and legs your animals have, the easier they are to join together. These funny frogs are decorated with pieces of colored paper glued to their backs.

Slithering snakes

Draw a snake with a curved neck and a loopy tail. Cut out and use as a pattern to make a lot more snakes. Give each one a face and decorate with stripes or triangles of paper.

Acro-cats!

To link a line of leaping cats, give each one a curly tail and carefully cut a little gap between their front paws. You can then hook the tail of each cat through the paws of the one above.

⚠ Ask an adult for help with this craft.

Tails and trunks

Elephants have tiny tails, so try hooking their trunks through a loopy back leg instead. Punch a hole and tie on some yarn to give each one a perky tail.

Crabby

The bendy legs on these crabs mean you can link them together in a lot of different ways. Try it with octopuses and spooky Halloween spiders, too.

Tip!

Try mixing up your animals to create a paper zoo! Link a snake to a monkey, then add an elephant or a frog to the chain, too.

Monkey business

Use arms and tails to make a string of funny monkeys. Cut their faces from a lighter paper color and draw on eyes, a nose, and a mouth with a marker.

31

Pots of fun

Give your coloring tools a nice new home with this fun pencil pot!

You will need:

- Cardboard container or can
- Thick paper
- Thin paper (colored and patterned)
- Scissors
- Double-sided tape
- Glue stick
- Ruler

1

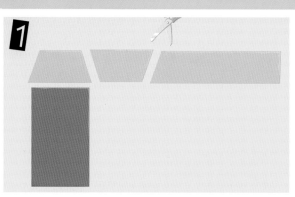

Cut a piece of thick paper the same height as your container and long enough to wrap around it. Cut out colored paper rectangles to make houses. Use a strip of paper for each roof, cutting the ends off at an angle.

2

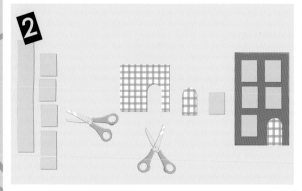

For windows and doors, cut smaller rectangles out of plain or patterned paper. Glue the pieces together to build each house.

3

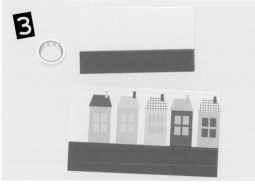

Glue a piece of paper along the bottom of the background strip to look like a street. Glue your houses above it, adding a roof and a paper chimney to each one.

4

Placing them a little bit lower down, glue another row of houses on top of the first one. Add roofs to each one, but no chimneys.

5

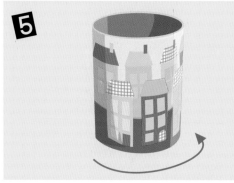

Wrap double-sided tape around the top and bottom edges of the container. Line up your picture and wrap it all the way around. Add extra tape to hold the paper ends in place.

Tip!

Use double-sided tape to stick the houses to the background, so the paper doesn't get crinkly and wrinkly!

Tip!

Try to make each house about half the height of your container.

All at sea

To make a sea pot for your pencils, cut and glue down wavy strips of blue paper. Cut out a white paper lighthouse and glue red stripes on top. Glue the lighthouse and a tiny paper boat to the waves, before wrapping the paper strip around your container, as before.

Make a note

Turn a plain notebook into a stylish scrapbook
or journal with these fun decorating ideas.

Fabulous fabric

Cut fabric from an old piece of
clothing and glue to the front
of your notebook. Fold over
the top, bottom, and right-hand
edges, then glue to the inside
of the cover. Hide the rough
edge on the left-hand side
of the fabric with a strip of
ribbon for a neat finish.

Tip!

Try to include a pocket when you
cut out the fabric so you'll have
somewhere to keep pens, pencils,
erasers, or other odds and ends!

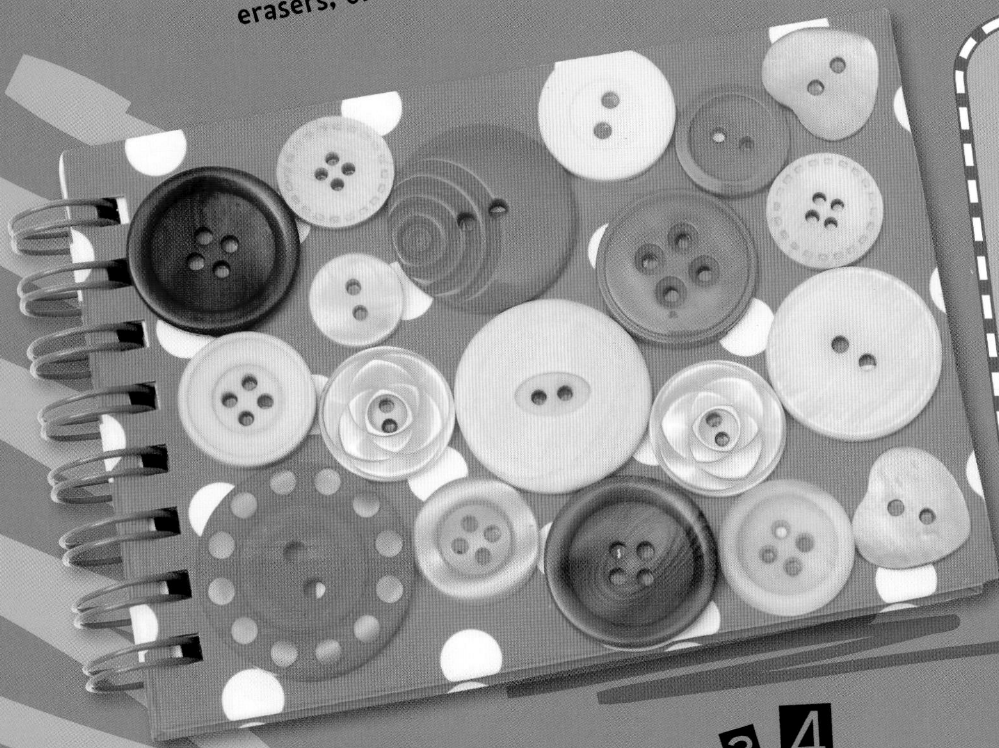

Button it!

Cover the front of
your notebook with a
lot of buttons. Stick
to just one color,
or use a mixture of
shades and sizes. Glue
the buttons down with
white glue, pushing
them together as
closely as possible.

It's a wrap

Glue a piece of wrapping paper to the cover, using a glue stick. Decorate it with strips of ribbon and curly string.

TIP!

This is a great way to recycle leftover gift wrap from birthday or Christmas presents!

Rip strips

Cover your notebook with plain colored paper. Tear more pieces of colored or patterned paper into strips. Glue them to the paper background to make straight or diagonal stripes.

That's handy

Brush paint onto your hands, one at a time, and carefully press down onto the notebook cover to make a print. Use different shades of paint and overlap the hand prints for a really cool, colorful look.

TIP!

Wash and dry your hands between paint colors, or your prints will be a mixed-up mess!

Easter egg-cellent

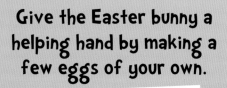

Give the Easter bunny a helping hand by making a few eggs of your own.

You will need:

- White glue
- Water
- Paintbrushes
- Craft paints or colored tissue paper
- Small bowl
- Old newspaper

1

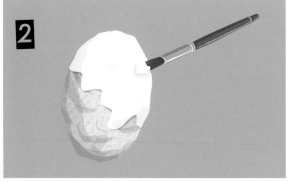

Mix some white glue and water in a bowl. Tear newspaper into pieces and soak in the glue mixture. Take the pieces out and mold into a smooth egg shape with your hands. Leave the egg somewhere warm to dry.

2

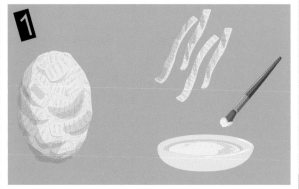

Decorate your egg with craft paints, or glue on pieces of colored tissue paper. Try brushing on a coat of plain white paint before you add the tissue so the newspaper underneath doesn't show through.

3

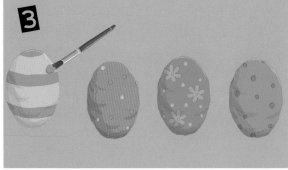

Add a pattern with more paint or pieces of tissue. Try some stripes, polka dots, flowers, or zigzags. Make as many eggs as you like, to fill an Easter basket.

TiP!

When you're making papier mâché, it's important to tear the newspaper strips. If you cut them, the pieces won't stick together as well, and your eggs will be lumpy on the outside!

TiP!

Make sure your eggs are completely dry before you paint them. If they're not, the paint will crack and peel off.

Egg hunt

Instead of just displaying your finished eggs in a basket, hide them around the house or yard for an Easter egg hunt.

Crazy cozies

Keep boiled eggs warm with one of these funny-faced egg cozies!

You will need:

- Thin cardstock
- Pen or pencil
- Scissors
- White glue
- Needle and thread
- Felt (various colors)
- Ruler
- Paintbrush
- Yarn
- Pins

⚠️ Ask an adult for help with this craft.

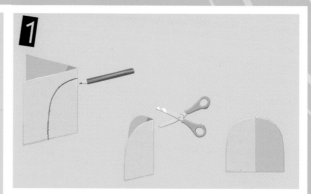

1

Fold a piece of cardstock in half and draw an arch shape, 3.5 inches high x 1.5 inches wide, to make a body pattern. Cut out and unfold. Trace around this pattern twice onto felt and cut out.

2

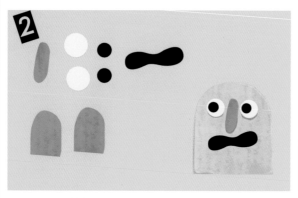

Cut more felt to make arms, eyes, a mouth, and nose. Glue the face to one of your felt body shapes and allow to dry.

3

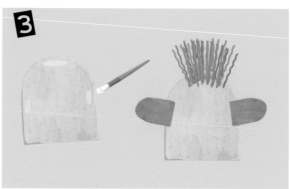

Spread glue onto the top and sides of the second piece of body-shaped felt. Glue on the arms and some short pieces of yarn to make hair.

4

To sew teeth, knot the end of your thread, then push the needle up through the felt near the edge of the mouth. Push it back through to make the first tooth. Repeat all the way around the mouth.

5

Pin the two felt pieces together with the hair and arms sandwiched in between. Sew together at the edges with a running stitch, leaving the bottom open for your egg!

TiP!

To make the hair, wind yarn around two of your fingers. Slide it off, then snip the loops so you have a lot of pieces the same length.

Twirly girl

Split or separate strands of yarn to make wild and fuzzy hair! Tie it into pigtails with tiny strips of ribbon.

Penguin pal

Glue on a triangular beak instead of a mouth and nose to create this cute penguin. Make his hair by snipping straight lines into an extra piece of felt.

Petal power

Add a flowery fringe by placing petal shapes between the two pieces of felt before you stitch them together.

TiP!

Remember to decorate the front before you sew the two pieces of your egg cozy together.

Love hearts

You are going to LOVE making these sweet stuffed heart decorations!

You will need:

- Thin cardstock
- Pen or pencil
- Pins
- Ribbon
- Felt (various colors)
- Ruler
- Scissors
- Needle and thread
- Cotton batting

! Ask an adult for help with this craft.

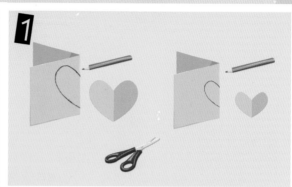

1 Draw half a heart onto folded cardstock and cut out. Make a smaller heart pattern in the same way. Trace around the large heart twice onto felt and cut out. Trace and cut out one smaller heart in a different color felt.

2 Pin the small heart in position onto one of the big hearts. Sew the small heart in place with running stitches around the edge.

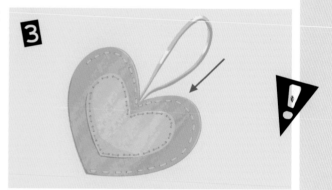

3 Fold a piece of ribbon in half to make a hanger. Pin the two large hearts together, with the ribbon ends sandwiched in between at the top. Sew around the edge, leaving a small gap for stuffing.

4 Push stuffing or cotton batting into the heart through the small gap, to make a nice rounded shape. Finish stitching to close up the gap. Sew over the last stitch a few times to stop it from unraveling.

Tip! Sew on a button or some sparkly beads for extra decoration. Remember to do this before stitching the two halves of your heart together.

Flower power

Cut out five felt petal shapes and sew into place on the first felt heart with one big stitch for each petal. Add a button to make the flower center, then sew the two hearts together as before.

Pretty patterns

Instead of felt, make a heart from patterned fabric, then cut out with pinking shears. This will stop the edges from fraying, and it looks pretty, too!

Felt friends

These fun hanging decorations are all made using the same idea as the stuffed heart.

TiP!
Use the same idea as the sun to make a roaring lion decoration!

Here comes the sun

Cut a big orange circle and a smaller yellow one. Using black thread, sew a face onto the small one. Stitch the two circles together, adding stuffing and a hanging loop as you go. Snip around the edge of the orange felt to make funky sunny rays.

Man in the moon

Draw and cut out two moon shapes. Sew them together at the edges and fill with stuffing. Use the ends of your thread to make a hanging loop. Draw on the eye and mouth with a marker.

Shining star

Make a simple star-shaped decoration and decorate by gluing on shiny sequins. Sew a button to the top of the star and knot the ends of your thread together in a bow, leaving a loop for hanging.

Jolly Roger

Cut two identical skull and crossbones from white felt. Sew together around the edges of the skull and fill with stuffing. Glue the bone pieces together and add a black hanging loop. Use a felt-tip pen to draw on the eyes, nose, and mouth.

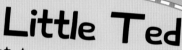

Hey, chick!

Cut out two circles of yellow felt to make a body. Add a tuft of hair and a ribbon loop to the back of the first circle of felt at the top. Stitch two buttons to the front to make eyes, then sew the circles together and add stuffing. Cut out a beak, wings, and feet, and glue into place.

Little Ted

Cut out two identical bear heads. Stitch together around the head, adding a hanging loop and stuffing as you go. Glue the ears together. Glue on extra pieces of felt for the nose, muzzle, and inside of the ears. Draw on a mouth and finish off with some googly eyes.

Monster fun

Stitch two monster shapes based on a circle together, adding a hanging loop and stuffing as you go. Glue on some felt spots and triangle-shaped teeth to decorate. Glue the eye stalks together, before adding some monster-ish googly eyes.

Jolly jellies

These bright and cheerful jellyfish will look awesome wiggling away on your bathroom mirror!

You will need:

- Thin cardstock
- Pencil
- Scissors
- Clear tape
- Glue dots
- Colored paper
- Colored pencils
- Googly eyes
- Yarn
- Ruler
- Double-sided tape

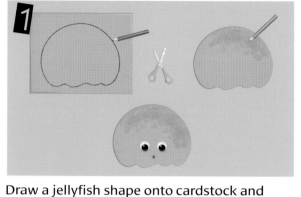

1 Draw a jellyfish shape onto cardstock and cut out. Shade around the edges with a colored pencil so it looks more realistic. Glue on some googly eyes and draw a mouth.

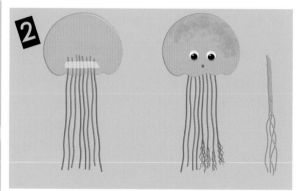

2 Cut pieces of yarn to make dangly tentacles for your jellyfish. Tape them to the back of the head. Twist and pull some of the yarn apart at the ends, to give it a wispy, wavy effect.

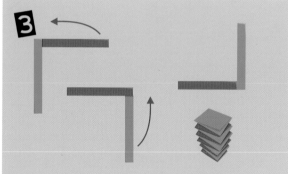

3 Cut two 12-inch strips of paper. Tape the ends together at right angles. Fold the bottom strip over the top one, lining up the edges. Repeat, and keep going until you've used up all the paper. Tape the ends down.

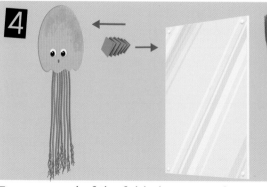

4 Tape one end of the folded paper to the back of your jellyfish's head. Stick the other end to the top of your bathroom mirror. The jellyfish should now look like it's floating and bobbing above the surface. Cool!

Tip!

Try using strips of colored plastic instead of yarn for another type of tentacle.

Take it Outside

Painted pots

Pretty up your flowerpots with these easy-to-paint decorations!

You will need:

- Terracotta flowerpot
- Craft paint (white, plus colors to suit your decorations)
- Paintbrushes (large or medium-sized for the background, small for decorations)
- Pencil

Paint your flowerpot white all over and allow to dry. Brush on a second layer of paint, in your chosen background color.

Draw your decorations onto the pot in pencil. Carefully fill them in with a small brush, one paint color at a time.

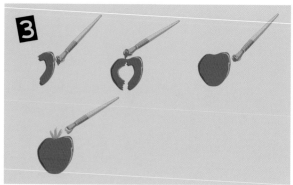

For the strawberries, paint a heart shape and add a green stalk. When the paint is dry, add yellow spots for seeds.

To paint simple flowers, start with five or six blobs of white paint to make petals. Allow the white to dry, then add a blob of yellow paint in the center.

Creepy crawlies

Cover your pot in brightly colored beetles! Start by painting oval shapes and allow them to dry. Then add two dots on top in different colors. Finish off with black painted heads, legs, and antennae.

Tip!

When all the paint is completely dry, brush a layer of white glue all over your finished pot. This will work like varnish and protect your painted decorations so they last even longer!

Tip!

Pick a light color for your background paint so the decorations on top will show up clearly and easily.

Sail away

For a summery seascape, start with a light blue background. Paint some boats on top in contrasting colors. Finish off with waves, clouds, and birds, painted in white and medium blue.

Cycle buddies

Jazz up the handlebars of your bike or scooter with these fun decorations!

You will need:

- Bowl
- Pencil
- White glue
- Colored cardstock
- Colored flexible straws
- Curling ribbon
- Clear tape
- Scissors
- Saucer

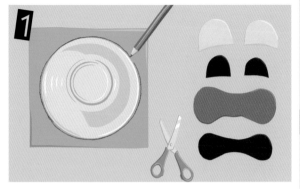

1 Trace a bowl shape onto cardstock and cut out. Pick a different color of cardstock and cut out big eyes and a monster-ish mouth.

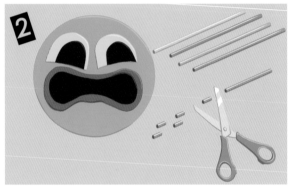

2 Glue the eyes and mouth to the circle to make a funny face. Be as silly as you like!

3 Cut straws into short pieces. Put some glue into a saucer and dip the straws in, one at a time. Glue them all over the face to decorate.

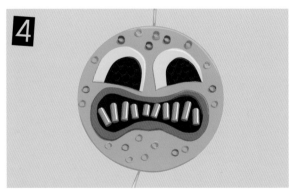

4 Tape a piece of curling ribbon to the back of the face, so you can tie it to your handlebars. Make a second monster in the same way, then tie both to your bicycle and ride with pride!

Tip!

Lay the pieces of straw flat over your monster's mouth to look like teeth. Stand the other pieces on their ends for a different effect.

Tip!

Glue pieces of straw side by side, alternating colors for a cute, striped look!

Flutter by

Cut out a butterfly from colored cardstock. Add pieces of straw to decorate the wings and body. Glue two flexible straws to the back for antennae.

Tip!

Use ribbon or plain string if you don't have any curling ribbon.

Christmas wreaths

Make these wreaths and then hang them up for some festive fun!

You will need:

- Thick cardstock
- Scissors
- White glue
- Green paper
- Small boxes or bundles of newspaper
- Christmas wrapping paper
- Pencil
- Clear tape
- Ribbon

⚠ Ask an adult for help with this craft.

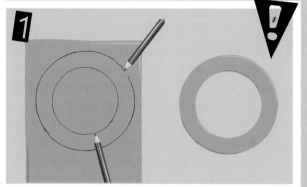

1 Draw a large circle on the thick cardstock and a smaller circle inside. Cut out the large circle. Make a hole in the small circle with a sharp pencil. Push your scissors through and cut out the inner circle, making a card ring.

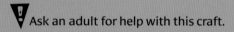
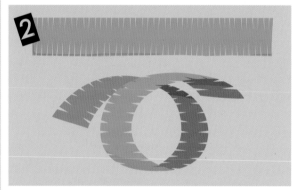

2 Cut out strips of green paper. Snip a fringe along both edges of each one. Curl up the fringes with your fingers to look like pine needles. Twist each strip into a loop.

3 Make tiny presents by wrapping small boxes or bundles of newspaper in Christmas paper. Glue them around the cardboard ring, gluing the green-paper pine needles in between.

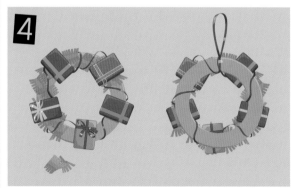

4 Wind some pretty ribbon around the ring. Fold it into a loop at the top to hang your wreath. Tape the ends neatly in place on the back.

Tip! Paint the cardboard ring to give your wreath a colorful background.

Cute as candy

Cut out candy canes from thick paper. Decorate them with a striped pattern, using ribbon, crayons, sequins, and markers. Cut leaf shapes from green paper and curl around a pencil before sticking to your wreath.

Tip!

To make the rings, trace around a dinner plate for the outer circle and a cereal bowl for the inner circle.

Tip!

Sprinkle glitter over the wet paint on your twigs to add some sparkle!

Let it snow

Glue real twigs around a cardboard ring and brush on white paint to look like frost or snow. Finish off with strips of festive red curling ribbon.

The garden gang

Get crafty in the yard or garden and make
yourself some cool new outdoor pals!

On the snail trail

Wash some old snail shells in soapy water and allow to dry. Wash your hands. Use your fingers to paint a face on each one. When the paint is dry, finish off the faces with felt-tip pens. Have fun adding different expressions to make all kinds of silly characters. Make absolutely sure the snail shell is empty before you wash it and start decorating.

⚠ Ask an adult for help with this craft.

Tip!

No googly eyes? No problem! Cut out circles of black and white paper and glue together. For a clear, glossy finish, brush white glue on top and allow to dry.

Pinecone friends

Break some twigs or sticks into small pieces and glue them to pinecones to make arms and legs. Use rubber bands to hold the sticks in place while the glue dries. Finish off by sticking two googly eyes to each pinecone.

Make characters using old wooden spoons. Tie a stick just below the round part of the spoon to look like arms, then try one of these fun decorating ideas ...

Spoon buddies

Cut a piece of fabric or old sock to make clothing for your spoon person. Decorate with ribbon or buttons. Draw a face on the top part of the spoon, and glue colorful plastic grass to the back to make hair.

Garden ghoul

Cut out two identical ghost shapes from white plastic (such as a plastic bag). Cut two small eye holes near the top of one and paint big, black eyes on the spoon to show underneath. Using double-sided tape, stick the ghosts together, sandwiching the spoon in the middle.

Trash-bag witch

Make a witch to go with your ghost. Paint the spoon and stick green, and then cut out clothes and a hat from a black trash bag. Try snipping zigzags along the edges and add a piece of string as a belt. Add some hair, too.

Chick sticks

To make a bird, paint the spoon first and draw on eyes. Add a beak using a piece of felt. Cut pieces of orange and yellow plastic with a feathery edge to make a body. Glue fluffy craft feathers to the back of the head.

TiP!

Set up a fun Easter treasure hunt by making a lot of chicks and hiding them in the yard. Add some tasty chocolate eggs at the end of the trail, too!

Windy wonders

Fold a few of these fun paper windmills and then head outside to get them spinning.

You will need:

- Flexible straw
- Colored paper
- Ruler
- Hole punch
- 2 rubber bands
- Double-sided tape
- Cardstock
- Scissors
- Pencil
- White glue

⚠ Ask an adult for help with this craft.

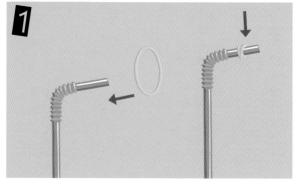

1 Bend the top of a flexible straw. Wrap a small rubber band around the short end a few times. Push it along so that it's just in front of the bend.

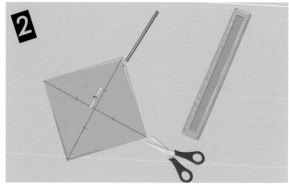

2 Cut out a 5-inch square of paper. Draw lines from corner to corner with a pencil and ruler. Starting at the center point, mark 1 inch along each pencil line. Cut along each line, from the outside corner to the mark.

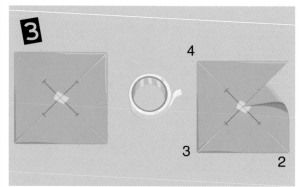

3 Stick a piece of double-sided tape over the center spot and peel off the backing. Take one corner of your square at a time and fold over so the point meets the center. Press down firmly onto the tape.

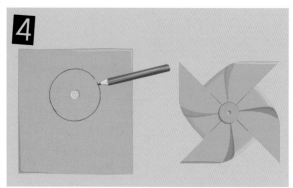

4 Punch a hole in a piece of cardstock. Draw a small circle around the hole and cut it out. Cover one side with glue and stick over the middle of your windmill. Allow to dry.

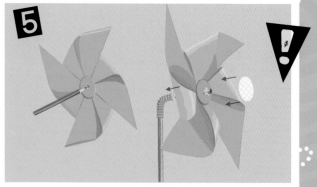

5 Push a pencil through the hole and pull out again. Slide the windmill onto the straw and add a rubber band in front to hold in place. Trim the straw in front of the rubber band and glue a circle of cardstock over the end.

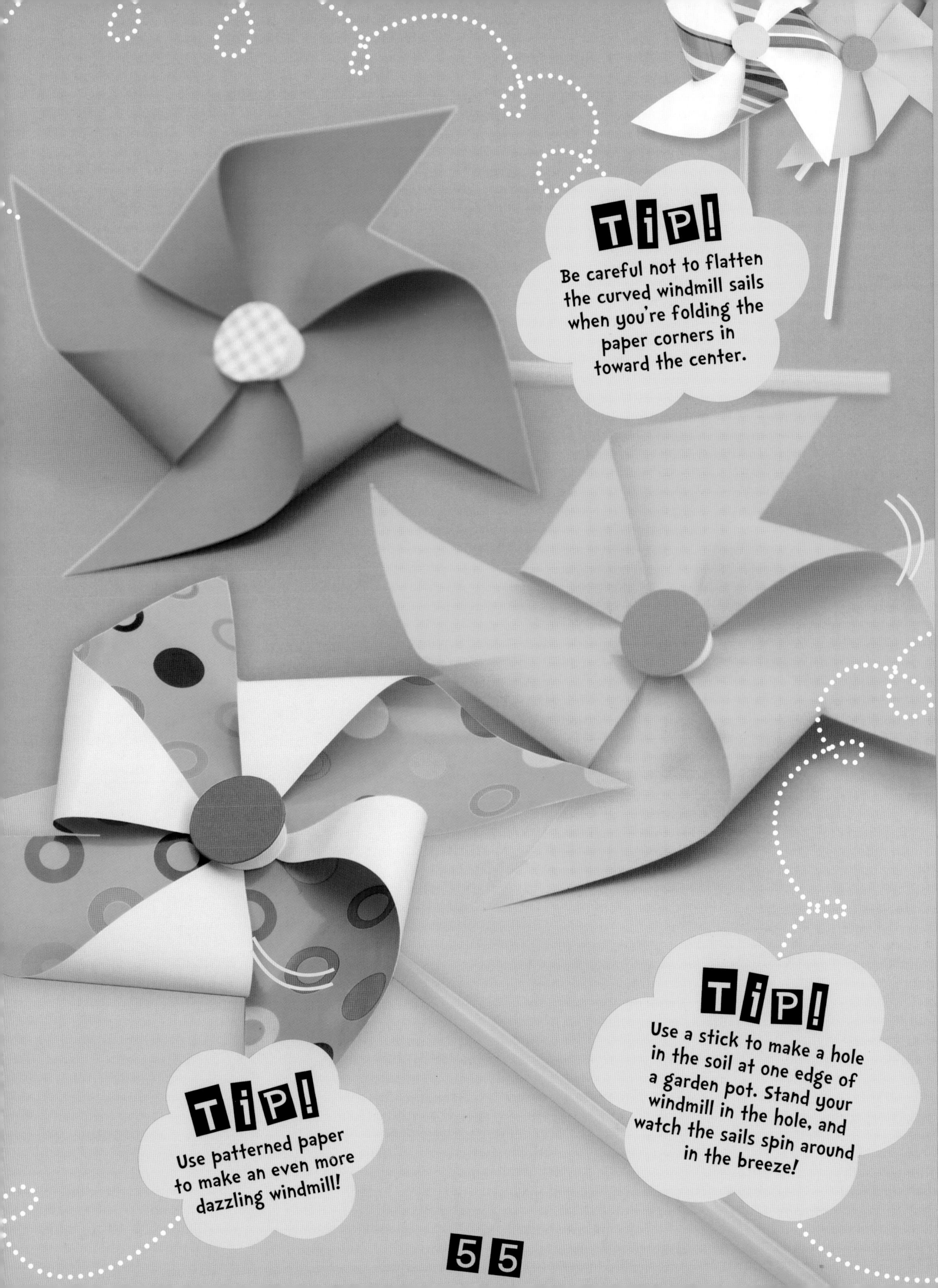

Tip!

Be careful not to flatten the curved windmill sails when you're folding the paper corners in toward the center.

Tip!

Use patterned paper to make an even more dazzling windmill!

Tip!

Use a stick to make a hole in the soil at one edge of a garden pot. Stand your windmill in the hole, and watch the sails spin around in the breeze!

More 'mills

Use the windmill instructions to help you make
even more wonderful whirligigs!

Double the fun

Glue two different pieces
of colored or patterned
paper together, back to back.
Use them to make sails for
your windmill, following
the instructions as before.
Glue a bead or sequin to the
cardstock circle in the center
for some added sparkle.

Catch a wave!

Instead of cutting straight
lines to make the sails on your
windmill, cut wavy ones! You can
do this either by moving the paper
as you snip or using decorative
scissors with a special wavy
cutting edge.

Tip!

To make a longer handle
for your windmill, cut
a slit at the end of the
straw. Add some glue
and push the end of
another straw inside as
far as it will go.

Paper-plate 'mill

Cut sections going in toward the middle of a paper plate, then twist over the edge of each section to catch the wind. Make a hole in the center and attach to a garden stick instead of a straw, using rubber bands as before. Push the end of the stick into the ground at an angle so your sails face the breeze.

Spinning flower

Cut each section of the paper plate into a petal shape so it looks like a flower. Don't forget to twist over the edge of each petal so your windmill catches the wind.

TiP!

Use pretty, patterned plates or decorate plain ones with paint.

Standing tall

To make a toy windmill, cover a cardboard chips tube with paper. Add a black paper door and windows. Use sharp scissors to make a hole near the top of the tube. Push a small pencil into the hole, leaving half an inch of the flat end sticking out. Glue into place. Make sails from a paper plate and rubber bands, as before. Add a circle of cardstock over the pencil end to finish off.

⚠ Ask an adult for help with this craft.

TiP!

Leave the lid on the tube so you can fill your windmill with pocket money, candy, or other tiny treasures!

Tree mobiles

Hang a string of homemade bugs from your favorite tree!

You will need:

- Colored cardstock
- Clear tape
- Glue stick
- Wrapping paper
- Colored string (or yarn)
- Scissors
- Pencil
- Sequins

1

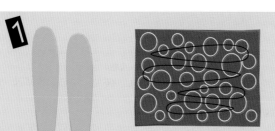

Cut out two dragonfly bodies from colored cardstock. Draw and cut out two big and two small wing shapes from patterned wrapping paper.

TIP!

If there are no trees in your yard, hang your mobile from a tall plant, balcony, or fence instead!

2

Glue the two big wings to the body, near the wide end. Add the small ones just below. Glue the second body on the first so the ends of each wing are hidden in between. Glue on two sparkly sequins as eyes.

3

Make more dragonflies in the same way. Tape them to a piece of colored string or yarn and then hang from a tree branch or tall plant.

Tip!

Use plain colored paper if you don't have any gift wrap for the wings. Try adding your own pattern with markers or glitter.

Bees in the trees

Decorate another mobile with busy bees and pretty flowers. Cut out a simple flower shape from cardstock and glue on a wrapping paper center. To make the bees, start with an oval-shaped body. Add stripes and tiny eyes using a black marker, then glue on patterned-paper wings.

Brilliant bunting

String up a garland of colorful fall leaves or painted paper veggies.

You will need:

- Paint
- Small dish
- Leaves
- Paintbrush or sponge
- Thick paper (in fall colors)
- Double-sided tape
- Cardstock
- Scissors
- Hole punch
- String

1 Mix some paint in a small dish. Place a leaf on a sheet of newspaper with the smooth side facing down. Brush (or sponge) paint all over the back of the leaf.

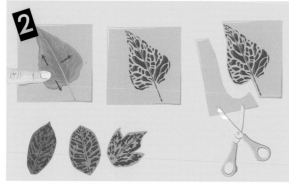

2 Place the leaf on colored paper, painted side down. Press firmly all over to transfer the paint. Use the stalk to lift the leaf away when dry. Cut out the printed leaf. Make more prints with other leaves and colors.

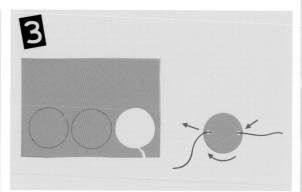

3 Count your leaf prints and cut out the same number of small circles from cardstock. Punch two holes in each circle, on opposite sides. Thread string in and out of the holes in the circles so they slide along the string.

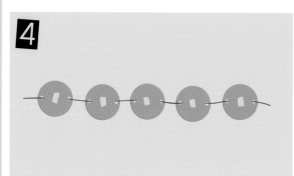

4 Stick a piece of double-sided tape to the middle of each circle. Press a leaf print down on top of each one.

5 Use the circles to slide the leaves along the string and arrange your finished fall garland!

Tip!

Make sure you don't stick double-sided tape over the string when you're attaching it to each of the circles.

Tip!

Don't let your paint get too wet, or the paper will curl up and make your finished garland wrinkly.

Squash up!

Draw and cut out some gourd or pumpkin shapes from colored paper. Decorate each one with crayons, then sponge on paint to make them look brighter and more realistic. String together to make a garland, as before.

String it up

Have fun making garlands or hangings that spin, twirl, flutter, and even jingle in the open air!

Cone-tastic!

Using plenty of white glue, stick three pinecones together, one on top of the other. Hold them in place with rubber bands while the glue dries. Fold a length of string or yarn in half and thread through a large bead. Tie a knot in the end, and then glue on top of the cones.

Nature chain

Cut a long piece of yarn and tie a knot near one end. Thread on a bead, push it right up to the knot, and tie another knot to hold it in place. Leave a gap, then tie on a pinecone. Keep going, adding beads and cones in the same way, until you've finished your garland.

Button chimes

Cut four or five long pieces of yarn and fold all in half. Knot together at the fold. Just below the knot, tape each piece to a bottle top, spacing them out evenly. Tie buttons along each length of yarn. Then hang up your decoration and listen to them jingle in the breeze!

Tip!

Wrap a strip of paper or ribbon around the bottle top to hide the tape and add a fancy finishing touch, such as beads, on the knot.

Fluttery streamers

Cut colored rectangle shapes from old plastic bags. Fold the top (short end) of each one over a piece of yarn and hold in place with tape. Cut each rectangle into narrow strips or streamers. Be careful not to cut through the yarn!

Stick tricks

Gather some sticks that are all similar in length. Fold a piece of yarn in half and tie a knot below the fold. Take a stick and tie the yarn around the middle. Wind the yarn around the middle of the next stick and tie a knot. Keep going until you've tied all the sticks together.

Spinning strips

Cut colored cardstock into strips. Lay the strips down, side by side, and add a blob of glue to the middle of each one. Place a piece of thread on top, pressing it into the glue, to join the strips together. Let dry. Then hang your spinner up and watch it blow in the breeze!

Tip!

Make sure the glue is completely dry before you try to pick up the spinner.

Flying the flag

Make a funky flag to fly in your backyard or wave when you are cheering for your favorite team!

You will need:

- Thick paper (three different colors)
- Ruler
- Pencil
- Scissors
- White glue
- Small brush or glue spreader
- Garden stake

1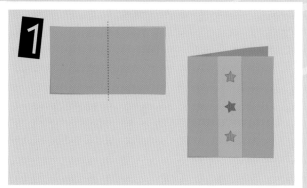

Cut a piece of paper, roughly 6 x 10 inches. Fold in half and crease firmly. Cut a strip of paper and some different colored stars, then glue onto the top flap.

2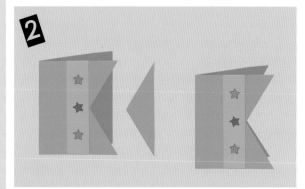

A little way in from the right edge, make a mark halfway down the flag. Cut a straight line from each corner to the mark. Fold the flag in half again. Copy the triangle-shaped cutout onto the back edge and cut out.

3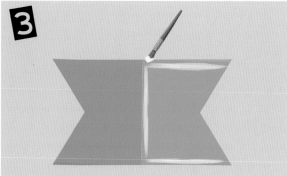

Open up the paper and place it face down. Add a line of glue just to the right of the center fold. Spread more along the top and bottom edges of the same side.

4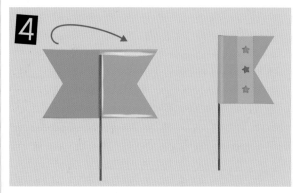

Place the garden stake on the glue along the center fold. Bring the left-hand side of the paper over so the points of your flag line up exactly. Press down to stick everything together.

Keep it simple

For an even easier flag, just fold over a plain rectangle shape. Try decorating it to look like the flag of your favorite country!

Ahoy there, matey!

Using black paper, tear the edges of your flag instead of cutting them. Don't make the shape too neat, especially at the ends. Paint on a skull and crossbones to finish off the perfect pirate flag. Arrrr!

TiP!

Make sure the decorated part of your flag is on the left-hand side, facing down, when you reach step 3—if it's not, you'll be waving a back-to-front flag!

Totally triangular

To make a triangular flag, fold a piece of paper in half. Mark the center point on the right-hand edge. Draw a straight line from the mark to the top and bottom of the central fold. Cut along the lines and repeat on the left-hand side. Glue and fold as before. Decorate!

Home sweet bug home

Help insects and birds feel at home in your yard
by making them somewhere special to live.

Stick stack

Gather up a bundle of small sticks. Tie them together with string and hang from the branches of a tree. If you're lucky, flying insects will use your bug home for nesting!

Insect heaven

If there's nowhere to hang a bundle of sticks in your yard, put them in a pot instead. Decorate an old food container and fill it with sticks. Creepy-crawlies will love using this as a place to hide and explore!

Nest-building bundle

Fill an old mesh onion or orange bag with bits of paper, cotton batting, small sticks, and pieces of grass. Tie the top of the bag with string. Hang it in the yard so birds can collect any of the bits and pieces they need for building nests.

Tip!

Make sure you don't put anything made from plastic in your net of goodies. Plastic won't break down and could litter the countryside.

Welcome to Bugtown!

To attract even more insects into your yard, make them a bug habitat. Collect old sticks, stones, and leaves, and pile them tightly in a corner. Then sit back and keep an eye out for signs of insect life!

Tip!

Ask a grown-up to help you find the best place in your yard for a bug habitat.

Home Sweet Home

Tealight fantastic

Place a small flashlight inside one of these gorgeous glass holders and watch them glow!

You will need:

- Tissue paper (various colors)
- Scissors
- White glue
- Paintbrush
- Ribbon
- Small glass or tealight holder

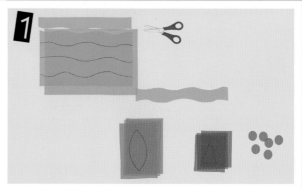

1 Cut blue and green tissue paper into strips with wavy edges. Cut out simple fish shapes in a different color. Make triangles for their tails and dots for eyes.

2 Brush glue all the way around the bottom half of the glass or holder. Press the tissue strips on top. Overlap the edges, so they look like waves in the sea. Add tissue strips to the top half of the glass in the same way.

3 Allow the glue to dry, then glue on the fish shapes, along with their eyes and tails. Space them out around the glass.

4 Snip off any rough paper edges. Glue a piece of ribbon around the top edge of the glass as a finishing touch.

These holders are not meant for real tealight candles. Instead, stand a small flashlight or battery-operated tealight in your glass. Just make sure it isn't raining when you put it outside!

TiP!

Sparkly ribbon looks especially good stuck around the top of your finished glass.

TiP!

Tissue paper is thin, so you can hold a few pieces together and cut through them all at once for quicker clipping!

Fold a butterfly

To make a perfect, neat butterfly, fold a piece of tissue paper in half and cut out a double wing shape against the fold. Open out the paper to reveal your butterfly. Glue to a decorated glass, with a body and some pretty spots on top. Add more butterflies to finish.

Bowling Pins

Paint a set of arty-smarty pins so you can bowl in your own backyard!

You will need:

- Plastic bottles
- Paintbrush
- Saucer
- Paint
- Kitchen sponges

1

Paint each plastic bottle in a bright color. You might need to brush on two or three coats of paint. Be sure to let each one dry before you add the next layer.

Tip!

Mix the paint with some white glue so it sticks better to the shiny plastic bottles.

2

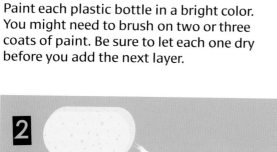

Cut shapes from a kitchen sponge. These will be used to make printed patterns. Note that you can print a square and a skinny rectangle from the same piece, by using the side edge, too.

3

Pour some paint into a saucer. Dip your sponge into the paint, then press it against the side of the bottle. Print a few more shapes in the same color. Allow to dry, then use a different color to fill in the gaps.

Tip!

You'll probably find it's harder to print on the sloping parts of your bottle. Try leaving them plain so you just decorate the flat section in the middle.

How to play:

Line up the pins in a triangle shape. Take four or five big strides away from them and mark a line or place a stick on the ground. Standing behind the line, roll a ball along the ground to try to knock over as many pins as you can.

Super Socks and fancy streamers

Grab some colorful plastic bags and make one of these awesome, windblown wonders!

Blast off!

Use plastic bags in different colors to cut out two identical rocket shapes, with flames at the bottom. Glue or tape the rockets together at the sides to make a tube. Add a length of thread at the top, then hang your rocket windsock out to flutter in the breeze!

Spooky spider

Draw and cut out a big, dangly spider! Give him eyes, tiny fangs, and long legs to blow in the breeze. Make two holes at the top, to tie on your hanging thread.

TiP!

If you're not confident cutting out a rocket shape, draw it on scrap paper first. Cut around your drawing and use it as a pattern to help you make the plastic version.

Two-color tube

Cut two rectangles from plastic bags the same length but one twice as wide as the other. Tape the bottom edge of the smaller one to the top edge of the wider one. Cut the wider rectangle into streamers, cutting from the bottom up to the tape. Wrap the smaller rectangle around a piece of cardboard tube and stick in place. Tie thread to the sides of the tube for hanging.

TiP!

Feeling funny? Hide your spider in a tree to give your friends a fright!

Crazy zigzags!

Cut out two identical rectangles from a plastic bag and tape the sides together to make a tube. Cut a curved shape at the top, then tie on some thread to make a hanger. Cut the ends of the windsock into strips, giving them zigzag edges.

Fluttering fish

Cut a fish shape from a plastic shopping bag. Stick a strip of double-sided tape along the bottom edge. Cut out long, thin strips from different colored plastic bags. Press the ends onto the tape. Make a hole at the top of the fish and hang it with a piece of thread.

Tip!

You can cut your streamer strips with straight edges or make them wavy instead.

Windsock it to 'em!

Cut a rectangle shape from a plastic bag and roll it into a tube shape. Stick the edges together with double-sided tape, leaving the bottom two-thirds free. Cut the bottom part into strips all the way around the tube. Tie some thread to the top, to hang your finished windsock out to blow in the wind!

Octo-streamer

Cut out an octopus shape from a plastic bag. Cut out two holes for eyes and glue or tape on streamers in two different colors. Add some beads to the hanging thread for extra fun!

Little bird

Say hello to a garden visitor who won't fly away, even in winter!

You will need:

- Cardstock
- Thin fabric
- Pencil
- Button
- Small brush or glue spreader
- White glue
- Scissors
- Felt
- Garden stake

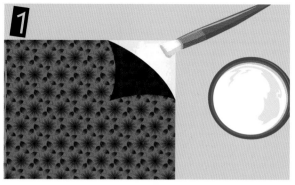

1 Brush glue all over a piece of cardstock. Place a piece of fabric on top and smooth it out with your hands to get rid of any creases. Allow this to dry.

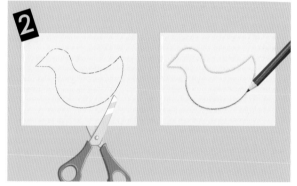

2 Turn the cardstock over so the fabric is facing down. Draw a simple bird on the cardstock and cut it out. Trace the shape onto another piece of cardstock and cut that out, too.

3 Take the fabric-covered bird and spread glue around the edges on the cardstock side. Leave a gap at the bottom. Press the second bird down firmly on top. Allow this to dry.

4 Cut a wing and beak from felt. Glue into place and stick on a button eye. Brush some glue around the top of a garden stake. Slide it into the gap at the bottom of the bird. Lie it down flat and allow to dry.

Party Pieces

Cupcakes and clowns

Get the party started with these fun and funky invitations!

You will need:

- Colored paper
- Pencil
- Scissors
- Paint
- Glue stick
- Ruler
- Markers
- Bubble wrap
- Paintbrush

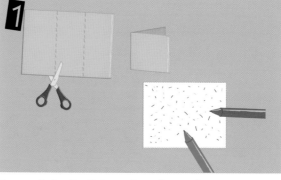

1 For each invitation, cut a piece of paper roughly 3.5 x 10 inches and fold it in half. Decorate another piece of paper with markers. Draw on a lot of dots and dashes to look like sprinkles.

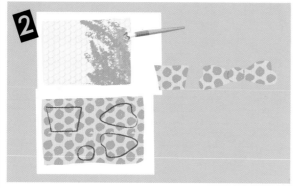

2 Brush paint onto the bubbly side of some bubble wrap. Press it down onto a piece of paper to make a dotty pattern, then allow to dry. Cut out a bow-tie shape and a cupcake liner.

3 Cut out frosting for your cupcakes from the sprinkles paper. Make extra cupcake layers, some cute cherries, an oval-shaped clown's face, a hat, hair, eyebrows, and a mouth from colored paper.

4 For the clown, glue the hair to your invitation first, then the face, the hat, the eyebrows, and the bow tie. Draw on eyes and cut out a dot from the bubble-wrap paper to make a nose. Glue a cupcake on another piece of paper in the same way.

Tip!

Add some sparkly swirls to your cupcakes with a gold or silver pen.

T!p!
Mix up the colors and shapes to make all your invitations look a little bit different.

T!p!
You should be able to make three invitations from a single sheet of letter-sized paper. Try cutting it exactly into thirds so you don't waste a scrap!

Name that bird

Help your party pals find their place with a festive bird name card.

You will need:

- Scissors
- Thick paper
- Double-sided tape
- Paper (light brown, dark brown, and red)
- Glue stick
- Marker

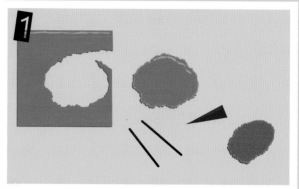

1 Tear a body shape from brown paper. Tear a small oval of red paper for the bird's breast. Cut out a dark brown paper triangle for the beak and two thin sticks for legs.

2 Glue the red breast, beak, and legs to the body. Draw on two tiny eyes with a marker.

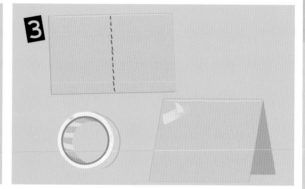

3 Fold a small piece of paper in half. Stand it up like a tent, with the fold at the top. Stick a piece of double-sided tape in one of the corners, near the folded edge.

4 Press your bird onto the double-sided tape to set it in place. Glue the legs on underneath its body. Neatly write the name of your party guest onto the card.

Tip! Mix up the paper colors to make different kinds of birds. Try gray for a gentle dove or blue for a vibrant bluebird.

Tip!

Make each of your birds look different by changing the position of their eyes and beak. Stick them to the place cards at different angles, too.

Tip!

Draw the outline of each bird shape on the back of your brown paper. Use the lines as a guide to help you tear out the pieces.

Sophia

Luke

Lily

Harry

Take your place

Turn plain plastic or paper cups into the fanciest party place cards!

Party princess

Paint a cup and turn it upside down. Stick on a paper face and arms. Decorate with a button or sequins. Cut a cone of paper into strands to make hair, then trim it so you can see the princess's face. Write your guest's name on a piece of paper, then roll it into a cone-shaped hat. Finish off with curling ribbon.

Good knight

Stick a ball of aluminum foil to the bottom of a plastic cup. Cover the whole thing in foil. Make a face, arms, breastplate, and shield from paper. Write your guest's name in the middle of the shield and glue it to one of the knight's hands.

Little monsters

Paint a monster onto a cup. Glue on paper arms. To make the flagpole, tightly roll up a piece of paper and glue the edge down. Tape a paper rectangle to the top. Cut out a "v" shape and add your guest's name. Glue to the monster's hand.

Tip!

Have fun mixing up your paint colors. Remember—monsters come in all different shades!

80

Cheeky monkey

Try making animal characters instead of paper cup people. Paint your cup a monkeylike shade of brown, then add a lighter color for the face. Draw on eyes, a nose, and a mouth, and finish off with some big paper ears.

Feathered friend

Stick a paper beak and wings to a cup that you've painted yellow. Give your chick a pair of googly eyes and stick a fluffy feather to the top of its head.

Ava

Mia

Cardboard cutouts

Cut a length of cardboard tube and paint it. Draw a face onto paper and stick to the front of the tube. Glue paper arms to the back, pointing forward. Cut the edges of a cupcake liner into a fringe for hair. Make a flag, as before. Stick to the hand, folding the fingers around the staff.

Tip!

Stir a little bit of white glue into your paint if it doesn't stick to the plastic cups very well.

Max

Emma

Tip!

Paper cups work just as well as plastic ones. Use whichever you can find at home.

Marvelous mats

Decorate your party table with these easy-as-pie paper mats!

You will need:

- Sheets of colored paper
- Pencil
- Scissors
- Markers
- Ruler
- Clear tape

1 Draw a line across the top of a piece of paper, 1 inch below the edge. Then, draw lines going in the other direction, 1 inch apart. Cut along each of these, up to the first pencil line.

2 Cut strips 1 inch wide from two sheets of different colored paper. Weave one of these through the strips on the first piece of paper—over, under, over, under. Push it up to the pencil line.

3 Add the next paper strip in the same way. This time, start your weaving by going under the first strip, then over, under, and so on. Keep adding more paper strips, alternating colors, until you reach the bottom edge.

4 Place a piece of tape along each side edge to hold the strips in place. Cut off any rough edges. Turn the mat over and draw funny faces or little cartoons in some of the squares to decorate.

Tip! Try using other materials to help you decorate the squares; maybe some glitter glue, stickers, stamps, or sequins.

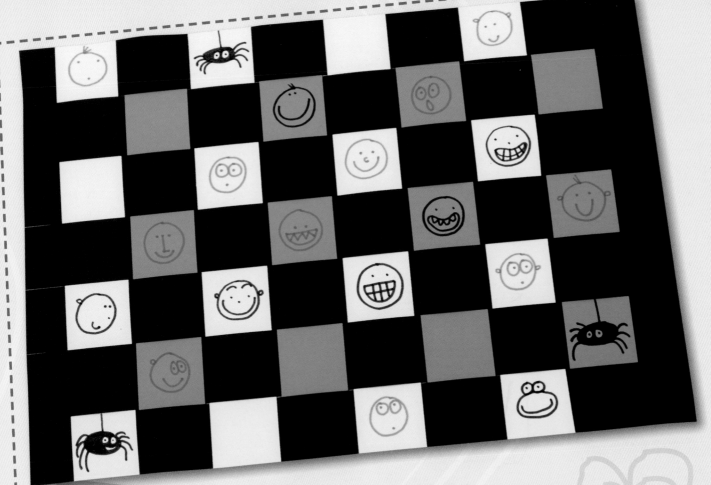

Paper blooms

Use different shades for your paper strips and then draw flowers in some of the squares using markers.

Fun and games

Have fun making and playing the coolest party games in town!

Pin the patch on the pirate

Draw a pirate face onto colored paper. Add a bright bandana but no eye patch. Cut out the face and make a separate eye patch.

HOW TO PLAY: Blindfold each player in turn and ask them to try pinning the patch on the pirate. The person who gets it nearest to the right place wins!

Tip!

Tack your pirate to a cork board. Push a pin through the eye patch. If you don't have a cork board, tape the pirate to a wall instead and stick a ball of sticky-tack to the back of the eye patch. Do the same with the tiger and its tail.

Stick the tail on the tiger

Draw and cut out the head and body of a tiger. Cut out a separate tail.

HOW TO PLAY: Blindfold each player in turn and ask them to try sticking the tail onto the tiger's body. The person who gets it closest to the right place wins!

Which leaf, which tree?

Collect some leaves from the yard or park. Paint each one and use it to make a print onto colored paper. Cut out and write the name of the plant or tree the leaf comes from on the back.

HOW TO PLAY: Hold up each picture and ask everyone to guess which plant or tree it's from. The person who gets the most right is the winner.

Tip!

Make a few prints from each leaf, instead of just one. Cut them out and use to play a leafy game of snap!

Musical islands

Cut some blob shapes from newspaper to make islands. Spread them out around the floor.

HOW TO PLAY: Play some party music and ask everyone to dance or walk around the room without stepping on the islands. When the music stops, players jump onto an island. The last one to make it is out!

Cup cuties

Add some personality to paper party cups with these fun toppers.

You will need:

- White cardstock
- Paper cups
- Colored pencils
- Markers
- Double-sided tape
- Pencil
- Scissors

1 Draw a frog's head onto white cardstock and cut it out. Color it in with a green pencil. Use markers to draw on eyes, a mouth, and two tiny dots for a nose.

2 Cut a rectangle out of cardstock, small enough to fit on the back of the frog's head. Fold outward to make a tab. Use double-sided tape to stick the flat top part to the back of the head, near the top of the frog.

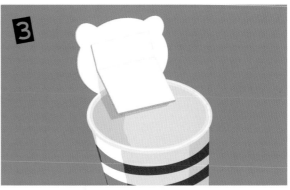

3 Slide the tab over the edge of a cup, so the frog is peering over the top. Make more smiley animals in the same way to cheer up your party drinks!

Tip! You shouldn't be able to see the tab from the front of your frog. If there are any pieces sticking out at the edges, you need to cut a smaller piece of cardstock.

Out of this world

Feeling silly? Add some weird and wonderful alien faces to get everyone giggling.

Fruity fun

Make some fruit-shaped decorations so your guests can tell what flavor their drinks are going to be.

Fancy straws

Slurp your party drinks in style through a cool, decorated straw!

You will need:

- Colored paper
- Pencil
- Scissors
- Double-sided tape
- Ruler
- Flexible straws

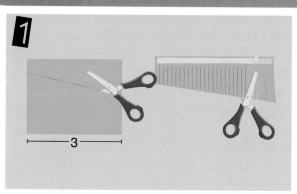

1 Cut a strip of colored paper 3 inches wide. Then, keep the top edge straight but cut the bottom off at an angle. Stick a piece of double-sided tape along the top. Cut a fringe into the sloping bottom edge.

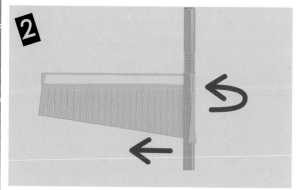

2 Peel the backing off the double-sided tape. Press the straw down onto the wide end of the paper strip with the paper just below the bendy part of the straw. Roll the straw along the paper, pressing onto the tape as you go.

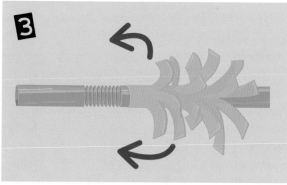

3 Use your finger to curl up the fringes. They should flick out and make a spiky decoration all the way around the straw.

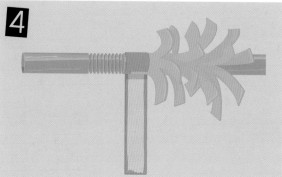

4 Stick double-sided tape onto a piece of paper in a different color. Cut out a thin strip. Wind it around the top of your paper fringe to finish off the decoration.

Sparkly sequins

Squeeze or brush small dots of glue onto a straw. Lie it down flat, then carefully press a sequin onto each dot of glue. Make sure the glue is dry before you use your sequined straw.

Spots, stripes, and squiggles

Draw a pattern of stripes, spots, or wavy lines onto a piece of paper. Cut out a 1.5-inch square and stick a piece of double-sided tape to the back. Press a straw onto the tape at one side of the square. Roll it along, so the paper wraps around the straw.

Go crackers

Everyone loves Christmas crackers—
why not try making your own?

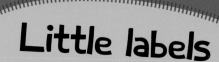

Let it snow

To make a cracker, start with a cardboard tube. Cut a piece of paper three times the length of the tube and wide enough to wrap all the way around. Roll the paper around the tube and glue in place. Scrunch the paper on either side of the tube and tie around the scrunches with ribbon. Cut out a paper snowflake to decorate the cracker. Add some sequins.

Little labels

Decorate your cracker with a pretty label. Cut a circle out of paper to match the paper you've used and glue a Christmassy shape on top. Try a star, a bird, or a cute candy cane.

Star bright

Cut a star shape from a kitchen sponge. Dip it in paint to stamp a pattern on brown paper. Add some paint dots with the end of a cotton swab. Let the paper dry, then use it to make your cracker. Tie the ends with plain string.

TIP!

Leftover wrapping paper is perfect for making crackers. You can recycle ribbon from presents, too!

Oh, Christmas tree!

Tie the cracker ends in place with curling ribbon. Cut out a Christmas tree shape to decorate the middle. Glue sequins to the tree, in colors that match the rest of your cracker.

Sparkly holly berries

Cut a fringe or some zigzags into the ends of your cracker to give it a feathered effect. Cut holly berries and leaves from paper. Decorate with white glue and sparkly glitter, then stick to your cracker.

Ding dong!

Use fancy ribbon to tie up the crackers and cut the paper ends into a wavy or zigzag shape. Cut out a gold bell and glue in place to decorate.

TiP!

After you've tied one end of the cracker shut, drop some goodies inside. You could add a joke, a tiny present, a paper hat, or maybe some fancy wrapped candies.

Sweet treats

Don't just eat the tasty
treats at your party—
hang them on the walls, too!

You will need:

- Colored cardstock
- Scissors
- Paint
- Paintbrush
- Brown cardstock
- White or cream cardstock
- Pencil
- Clear tape
- Glue stick
- Thread

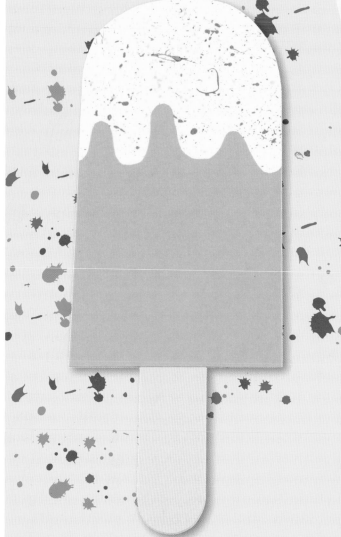

1

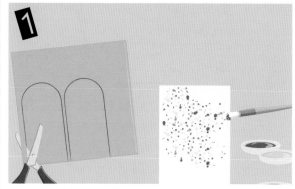

Cut two identical ice pop shapes from colored cardstock. Splatter paint onto some white or cream cardstock so it looks like it's covered with sprinkles.

2

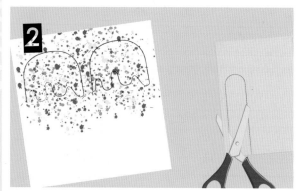

Draw two pieces to fit over the top of your ice pop, with dribbly, wavy edges at the bottom. Cut both out of the decorated white cardstock. Cut out an ice pop stick shape from brown cardstock.

3

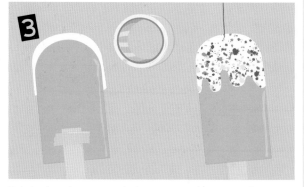

Stick the decorated shapes to the top of your ice pop. Turn one over and tape the brown stick to the bottom. Tape a loop of thread at the top for hanging. Glue the second ice pop on top to make a double-sided decoration.

Tip!

Draw and cut out the main shape, then trace around it onto some more cardstock. When you cut out the second shape, it should be exactly the same as the first one! Do the same to make your topping pieces identical, too.

Lovely lollipop

Cut out circles of cardstock to make a tasty-looking round lollipop. Cut out a spiral of cardstock in a contrasting color and glue it on top. You could try tracing around the spiral with a line of sparkly glitter, too.

Tip!

For the paint splatters, mix some water into your paint so it splatters more easily. Don't forget to put old newspapers or a plastic sheet underneath, too. Splattering is fun but messy!

Ice cream sundae

Why stop at an ice pop when you can make a whole bowl of yummy ice cream? Cut out circles of cardstock to make the ice cream. Add dots to one of the scoops using paint and a cotton swab. Make a sundae bowl with colored cardstock and decorate with paint.

Chain chums

Have fun decorating your house with these cool party paper chains.

Go loopy!

Cut patterned paper into strips. Curl one of them around into a loop. Stick the ends together. Take the next strip and slip it through the first one. Curl into a loop and stick the ends together. Keep adding strips in the same way to make a long chain.

On the edge

Paper chain strips can be cut with a straight edge, a wavy edge, or a spiky, zigzag edge. You could even link a mixture of all three.

Take the cake

Thread a long piece of string or yarn onto a needle. Push through the middle of a cupcake liner, then tie a knot. Add another cupcake liner and tie another knot. Keep adding liners, using the knots to keep them spaced evenly apart.

Tip!

Give your chain of cupcake liners a striped look by alternating between different colors.

Little lanterns

Thread cupcake liners onto a piece of string so they face in different directions: forward, backward, forward, backward. The liners will make lantern shapes along the string. Add spots of glue around the edges to gently stick each pair together.

Jingle bells

Cut out circles of cardstock and punch a hole in each one. Tie one of the circles to a piece of thread and make a knot 1 inch above. Use a needle to push the thread up through a cupcake liner. Tie the end to a piece of string. This makes one bell. Add more bells along the piece of string to make a jingle-bell banner.

Everlasting daisy chain

Cut out a bunch of big daisies from colored cardstock. Make a slot at the end of each stem, using scissors. It should be wide enough for another stem to fit through. Slide the stems together, just like you would if you were making a real daisy chain.

! Ask an adult for help with this craft.

Tip!

Add as many daisies to your chain as you like. Make it short and sweet or long and fabulous!

Hat tricks

Try some simple paper folding and turn your party guests into Mad Hatters!

You will need:

- Pencil
- Scissors
- Glue stick
- Colored paper
  (letter-sized plus scraps)

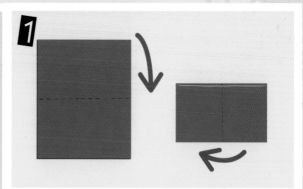

1 Fold a large piece of paper in half widthwise. Fold it in half again to make a crease down the middle. Open out the second fold and smooth it flat.

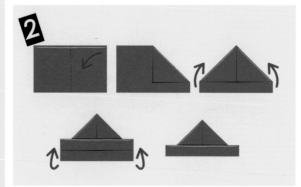

2 Fold the top right corner over so the top edge meets the center crease. Press firmly along the fold. Do the same on the left-hand side. Fold the front bottom piece upward. Turn the paper over and turn the final bottom up.

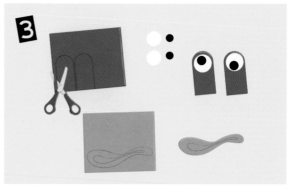

3 Now that you have your basic hat, decorate it! Cut two small arch shapes the same color as your hat. Glue black and white circles to the end of each one to make monster eyes. Cut out a funny mouth.

4 Stick one eyestalk to each side of your hat, just behind the diagonal edges. Glue the mouth to the front. Finish off with two small black circles to make a nose.

Tip!

Try folding hats from different types of paper. Leftover gift wrap works well, and pages from old comics can be fun, too.

Paper blossom

For a style that's simple but pretty, cut out a big paper flower and stick it to the brim of your hat.

Tip!

If you prefer, you can stick the eyes right onto the front of the hat, instead of adding eyestalks. Make them big and googly!

Ship shape

How about a hat that looks like a boat? Use scraps of colored paper to make sails and a flag, then stick on circles for the portholes. All aboard!

Make a mask

Why not give your party a dress-up theme and wear
one of these amazing masks!

⚠ Ask an adult for help with these crafts.

Flower fairy

Draw around a pair of your glasses
or sunglasses to make a basic
mask pattern. Copy this onto pink
cardstock and cut out. Make eye
holes, then decorate the mask with
flowers and sparkly sequins. Tape
pieces of ribbon or thread to the
back of the mask on each side. Tie
them together at the back of your
head to hold the mask in place.

⚠ TIP!

Draw eyes on your mask, then make a hole
in the middle of each one with a sharp
pencil. Push scissors through to cut out
each of the eye holes.

Mask-o-saurus

Trace around your mask pattern to make
a dinosaur face. Cut out a frill
from a different cardstock color and
stick it behind the face. Cut out two
horns, a nose, and spots to decorate.
Glue into position. Make your eye
holes using the tip above.

Cool kitty

Using the mask pattern as a guide,
draw the top of a cat's face and
cut it out. Stick on triangles
inside the ears and a heart for
the nose. Add some sequins to each
cheek and tape on curling ribbon
to make whiskers. Make your
eye holes carefully.

Knight time

Draw a pointy knight's helmet around your mask pattern and cut out. Cut slits for eyes so they look more menacing. Using a different color, add a nose guard and ear flaps at the sides. Glue buttons across the middle to look like studs.

Tip!

To make the helmet look more like real metal, cut some of the pieces from foil.

Dragon danger

Add big ears to each side of the basic mask outline, then cut out the whole shape. Glue circles of colored paper over the eyes to make them look bigger. Cut out the eye holes, cutting through both layers. Stick horns to the back of the mask to finish off.

Bird is the word

Cut out a basic mask shape and add a beak near the bottom. Glue a row of feathers along the top of the mask. Decorate with colorful sequins. Make your eye holes carefully.

Beautiful butterfly

Using your mask pattern as a guide, draw and cut out a butterfly shape. Cut eye holes. Decorate with extra pieces of colored paper and add sequins or tiny jewels as a fancy, sparkly finishing touch.

Goodie bags

Make your own party bags and fill them with cool stuff so everyone goes home happy!

You will need:

- Ruler
- Scissors
- Green paper (letter-sized)
- Scraps of colored paper
- Pencil
- Double-sided tape
- Marker

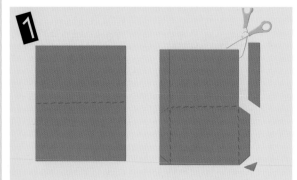

1 Fold a piece of green paper in half and open it out again. Mark 1 inch along each side edge. Cut off the edges from the top half. Cut a small triangle in each bottom corner and one near the center line on each side.

Tip!

Draw around a plate to make a nice curved, smiley mouth. Use smaller objects, such as bottle tops or egg cups, to trace circles for the eyes and nose.

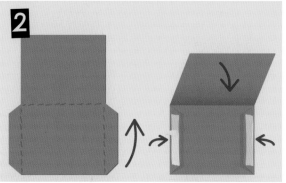

2 Fold the side edges inward. Stick a strip of double-sided tape to each one. Fold the top half of the paper over and press the side edges onto the double-sided tape. You've made a bag! Turn it open side up.

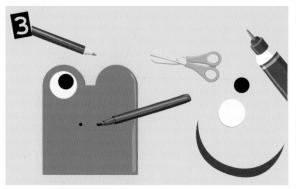

3 Draw big circles at the top. Cut around them, then cut away the middle so your bag starts to look like a frog. Stick on pieces of paper to make eyes and a smiley mouth. Draw on dots for a nose.

Paper shaper

For a super-simple bag, glue on a paper shape to the basic bag, such as a flower or a star. Stick some curling ribbon on the flower to add extra detail. Cut a pattern across the top of the bag.

Fancy patterns

Patterned wrapping paper makes great party bags. Cut and fold it to the size you want, then cut out fun shapes along the top edge. Make a hole in one corner and tie a piece of curling ribbon through it to make a handle.

Tip!

You can use any kind of wrapping paper, from pretty flowers to cool cartoon designs!

101

Thanks a million

Saying thank you is loads of fun with these cool cards.

You will need:

- Glue stick
- Markers
- Ruler
- Colored paper (including cream and red)
- White paper
- Scissors
- Pencil

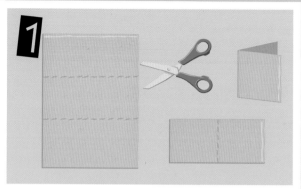

1 Cut a piece of paper roughly 3.5 x 8 inches. You should be able to make three of these from a single sheet of letter-sized paper. Fold the piece in half.

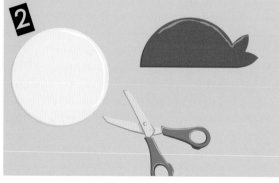

2 Cut out a small circle of cream paper. Draw another one the same size onto red paper. Mark a line across the middle of the red circle. Add two loop shapes at one side. Cut out the bandana shape with the loops.

3 Stick the red bandana onto the cream circle. Draw on a pirate's face. Add an eye, eye patch, mustache, mouth, and a dotty, stubbly beard.

4 Tear a piece of white paper to fit on the front of your folded paper. Stick in place. Glue the pirate to one corner. Write "Thank you" on the front and add a special message inside.

Tip! Trace around an egg cup or small lid to make perfect circles for your pirate's head and bandana.

All at sea

Cut out some waves, a ship, and a few circling seagulls to decorate your card. Write your thank you message on the sails or across the deep blue sea.

TiP!

The torn paper on the front of the card looks like an old treasure map. See if you can make your writing look old and pirate-y to match!

Up, up, and away

Use colored paper or fabric to make a kite and cloud. Use stickers or your best handwriting to add a message in the fluffy white clouds.

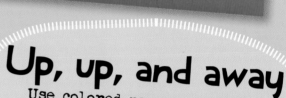

Thank You

Christmas coasters

Stand your festive party drinks on one of these fun paper coasters.

You will need:

- Colored cardstock
- Mug
- Shiny paper
- Glitter
- Drinking glass (or something similar)
- Pencil
- Scissors
- Glue stick

TiP!
Use red and green cardstock for an extra-festive look.

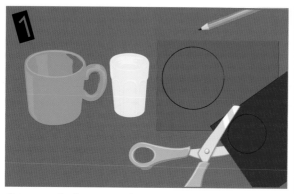

Draw a circle around a mug onto colored cardstock. Pick a different color and draw around something a bit smaller than the mug, such as a drinking glass. Cut out both circles.

Draw and cut out a star pattern. Trace around the pattern onto shiny paper and cut out. You'll need to make three or four stars for each coaster.

Spread glue around the edge of the biggest cardstock circle. Sprinkle glitter on top and allow to dry. Stick the smaller circle in the middle and glue stars on top to decorate.

Give a Gift

Music monster

Help a friend keep their music or video game player safe inside this funny monster!

You will need:

- Felt (various colors)
- Pencil
- Scissors
- Needle
- Embroidery thread
- Ruler
- Pins
- Buttons

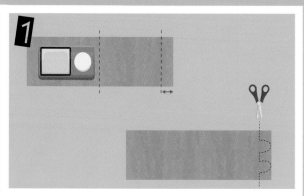

1 Cut a piece of felt a bit wider than your music player and twice the length of the player, plus an extra inch or so. Cut out eye shapes at one end.

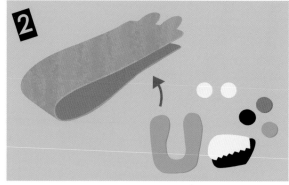

2 Fold the felt over so the edges line up and the eyes stick out at the top. Mark the position of the bottom edge with pins. Cut out a mouth, teeth, and two white circles for eyes. Cut out extra circles in fun colors.

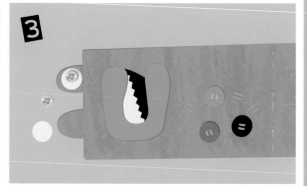

3 Unfold the felt and sew one white circle and a button over each eye. Stitch the mouth into place below. Add the colored circles between the mouth and the row of pins. Sew extra stitches around them to decorate.

4 Fold the felt in half again and take out the pins. Sew each side edge together using a running stitch.

Tip!

If you don't have a music or video game player, use your monster as a pencil case instead.

TIP!
Put the teeth under the mouth so you can sew both pieces to the case with just one set of stitches.

TIP!
It's all right if your sewing isn't very neat. Monsters often look a bit messy!

Charm School

Hang one of these cheery charms from a music player, pencil case, or backpack!

You will need:

- Thin cardstock
- Scissors
- Needle and thread
- Ribbon
- Stuffing or cotton batting
- Pen or pencil
- Felt
- Tiny beads

1

Draw a star onto a piece of cardstock and cut it out. Trace around it twice onto felt. Cut out the two felt stars.

Tip!

To sew on a bead, push the needle through the felt, from back to front. Then, thread it through the bead, and back down through the felt. Do this a few times, to make sure it's fixed firmly in place.

2

Sew a mouth onto one of the stars, using a running stitch. Stitch two tiny beads into place as eyes.

3

Fold a piece of ribbon in half and place the ends between the two felt stars. Sew the stars together at the edges, stitching over the ribbon to hold it in place. Leave a small gap and push some stuffing inside. Stitch the gap shut to finish.

Scrumptious strawberry

Cut two strawberry shapes from red felt and two spiky leaf pieces from green. Add some extra stitches around the front to look like strawberry seeds.

Monster mate

To make a charming monster, cut out two circles and four strips to make legs. Cut along the bottom of each strip with pinking shears. Sew on some zigzag teeth, too!

Tip!

Scissors with a zigzag edge are called pinking shears. If you don't have any, snip zigzags with a small pair of normal scissors instead.

Charm-bot

Cut out a square robot head and two rectangle-shaped ears. Cut out an extra strip of felt using pinking shears and sew it on to make a mouth. Finish the bottom of the robot with zigzags.

Jazzy jewels

Whip up some snazzy jewelry for someone special, or keep it all for yourself!

Friendship braids

Cut six pieces of yarn, all the same length. Tie together 3 inches from one end. Divide into three and start to braid. When the braid is long enough to wrap around your wrist, tie another knot. Cut off the ends, leaving enough spare yarn to tie the bracelet in place.

HOW TO BRAID:

Split your yarn or thread into three equal groups. Move the group on the left over the one in the middle and tighten. Then, move the group on the right over the one in the middle and tighten. Do the same again and again until your braid is the right length.

Tip!

To make a chunkier bracelet, start with 9, 12, or even 15 pieces of yarn.

Brilliant beads

Thread beads onto a length of string, ribbon, or yarn. You can leave gaps between each one or push them more closely together. Tie a knot at each end to hold the beads in place. Leave enough string or ribbon to tie the bracelet around your wrist.

Loopy bangles

Cut loops of paper towel roll with a straight or wavy edge. Paint and allow to dry. Decorate with sequins, ribbon, or marker drawings. If the paper towel roll is too tight, snip through it so you can easily slide the cardboard bangle on and off your wrist.

Give me a ring

Cut a strip of cardstock big enough to wrap around your finger. Curl it around into a loop shape and stick the ends together. Glue on a button or a small shell to decorate.

Bottle-top treasures

Fill an old bottle top with white glue. Sprinkle on some glitter or press tiny beads and sequins into the glue. Stick a loop of cardstock to the back to turn it into a ring. Or, to wear it as a brooch, fix a piece of double-sided tape to the back.

Tip!

If the double-sided tape isn't sticky enough after you've worn your brooch a few times, just add a new piece on top!

Buttons and bows

Thread a button onto a length of narrow ribbon and tie a knot. Do the same with another button. Keep going until the button-decorated part of the ribbon is long enough to go around your wrist or neck. Tie the ribbon ends in a bow to hold in place.

Join the band

Cut strips from old socks or pairs of tights. Wear them as colorful wristbands!

Juggly socks

Give someone the gift of juggling with these fun balls, made from mismatched socks.

You will need:

- Socks
- Scissors
- Dry (uncooked) rice
- Rubber bands
- Needle and thread

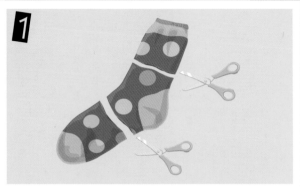

1 Cut across a sock just above and just below the heel. You only need the toe and leg sections to make a juggling ball.

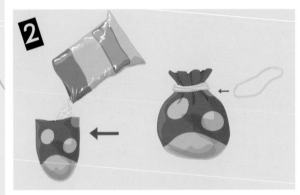

2 Pour rice into the toe section until it's about half full. Scrunch the top together and twist a small rubber band around it to hold shut.

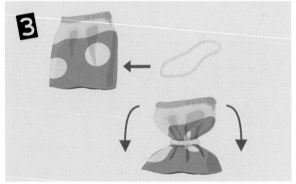

3 Turn the leg part of your sock inside out. Twist a rubber band around the middle a few times. Roll the top down so the right side is showing again. You should now have a little hat shape.

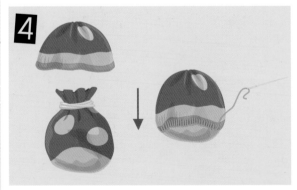

4 Put the hat over the rice-filled sock and pull it down. Sew the two pieces together around the bottom edge.

Tip!

You can make two juggling balls from one pair of socks. To juggle with three balls, you'll need two pairs. If you have any mismatched socks, it's even better—make one ball from each sock!

Tip!

You can make juggling balls from longer socks, too. Just snip off the toe section (as above), then cut a piece from the top of the leg that's the same length.

Tip!

Don't throw away the heel of your sock. You might be able to use it in another craft project!

Keepsake wallet

Make a neat envelope for storing special letters, cards, and photographs.

You will need:

- Ruler
- White glue
- Old map pages
- String
- Paper (letter-sized)
- Scissors
- Photograph
- Pinking shears

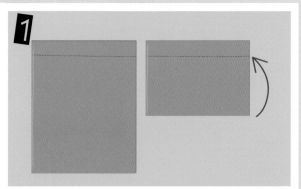

1 Fold over roughly an inch along the top edge of your paper. Press firmly to make a crease, then unfold again. Fold the bottom end over, and line up the edge with the crease you've just made.

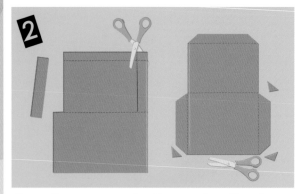

2 Open the paper again. Cut a strip off each side of the paper with the folded end, from the top edge down to the fold in the middle. Clip a triangle off each corner.

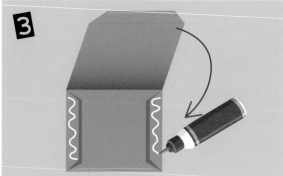

3 Fold over the side edges in the bottom half of the paper. Spread glue on each one. Fold over the top half of the paper and press the edges firmly down. Turn so that the open edge is at the top and the flap points back.

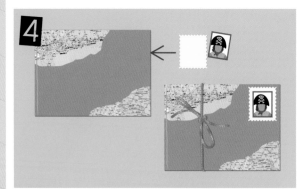

4 Decorate the corners of the wallet with pieces of an old map. Use a photograph and pinking shears to make a stamp. Tie string around the middle of the wallet so you can keep things safe inside.

Tip! If you don't have a photograph to use for your stamp, cut one out of a magazine. Stick it onto a spare piece of paper, so it's easier to cut the zigzag edges.

Firm favorites

Decorate the front of an envelope with pictures of your favorite things. Cut them out of magazines or draw them on yourself. Tie the envelope shut with a piece of fancy ribbon instead of string.

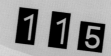

Wonderful weaving

Weave your way in and out of these fun ideas!

Fancy square

Fold a piece of colored paper in half. Cut slits into the paper from the fold toward the opposite edge. Leave a small border all the way around. Unfold the paper and weave strips of tissue paper in and out of the slits. Try weaving a piece of thread, too, and add some beads as you go.

Tip!

Use strips of silver curling ribbon to make your weaves really shine!

Up a notch

Cut small triangle-shaped notches along the top and bottom of a piece of paper. Tape a long piece of ribbon to the back of the paper next to a corner notch. Wind the ribbon around the paper, using the notches as a guide. At the last notch, tape the ribbon to the back to hold in place. Weave fabric strips in and out across the vertical strips of ribbon and stick any ends to the back for a neat finish.

Pretty in plastic

Fold a piece of plastic bag in half. Cut slits into it, as before. Weave thin strips of plastic in and out of the slits. Use clear tape to hold the ends in place.

TiP!

Try mixing up the colors of your plastic strips for a more interesting look.

Pull shapes!

Make a woven square, using colored paper and strips of leftover wrapping paper. Cover the back with clear tape to keep all the pieces in place. Draw a shape (such as a star or circle) on the front in pencil and cut out.

TiP!

Hang your weave on the wall or lay on a coffee table for decoration.

Fantastic fabric

Weave fabric through strips of ribbon or yarn, as in "Up a notch." Then snip through the ribbon or yarn at the back of the paper about halfway down. Tie the loose ends of ribbon or yarn at the top of your weave around a straw. Do the same at the bottom. Add a loop of yarn to the top straw as a hanger.

Bowled over

Use tiny bits of tissue paper to turn a plain bowl into a work of art.

You will need:

- Tissue paper
- White glue
- Paper bowl
- Scissors
- Brush

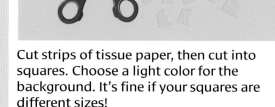

1

Cut strips of tissue paper, then cut into squares. Choose a light color for the background. It's fine if your squares are different sizes!

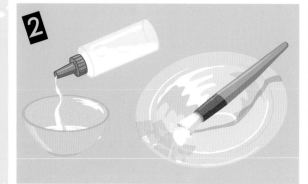

2

Pour some glue into your bowl, then brush it all over the inside. Paste tissue paper squares on top. Overlap the edges of each square and let the pieces go over the rim, too.

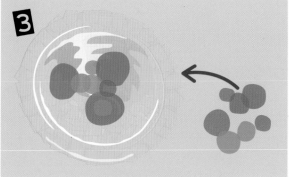

3

Cut circles out of tissue paper in a few contrasting colors. Make the circles different sizes. Glue to the background, overlapping some of the circles to add new colors and shapes to the design.

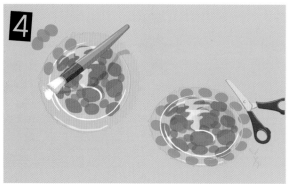

4

Paste some extra circles around the rim of the bowl to finish off. Make sure they don't go over the edge. Allow the bowl to dry, then trim off the rough edges with scissors.

Tip!

Colors can sometimes run when you use bright shades of tissue paper. To avoid nasty splatters, let the background dry before you stick the circles on top.

Super-stripes

After finishing the background, stick thin strips of tissue paper down in a cross shape. Add another cross on top, then stick strips in between to make an even, striped pattern.

Tip!

For an even more special present, fill the bowl with wrapped candy and decorate with a fancy ribbon. Don't eat from it, though. These bowls are only made to hold pretty things!

Try a triangle

Make your background out of triangular pieces of tissue paper. Then stick brighter triangles around the bowl's edge, with the corners lined up to make zigzags. Add more triangles in the middle, pointing inward, for a sharp design.

119

Papier mâché marvels

Try out the marvelous art of papier mâché
with these fun—and easy—ideas.

Bowl bling

Cover the inside and the top edges of a bowl with a piece of plastic wrap. Tear wrapping paper into strips. Dip into a mixture of half white glue and half water. Paste strips on top of the plastic wrap, overlapping the edges as you go. Add four or five layers in the same way. Allow to dry. Pull on the edges of the plastic wrap to lift the papier mâché out of the bowl, then peel off the cling film.

Lovely leaves

Start making a bowl with tissue-paper strips. After you've stuck down two or three layers, try adding some leaves. Dip them in the glue and water mixture, then smooth over your paper. Add one more layer of tissue strips on top, then allow to dry.

Scrunch it!

Make a papier mâché bowl, as before, but try scrunching the paper strips before you stick them into place. This will give your finished bowl a fun, wrinkled effect.

Cute like a cookie cutter

Line the inside edge of a cookie cutter with plastic wrap. Soak strips of paper in a mixture of half white glue and half water for a few minutes. Scoop the pieces out and squeeze gently. Press the mixture into the cookie cutter with your fingers. When dry, carefully take the cutter and plastic wrap away.

Tip!

Use paper from old comics or magazines to make cool, multicolored shapes.

Sequins and beads

Add beads or sequins to your papier mâché as you press it into cookie cutters. When the glue mixture is dry, they'll be fixed in place, along with the paper.

Glittery mâché

Stir some glitter into the bowl with your glue and water. Use it in any of your papier mâché projects to make them sparkle.

Tip!

Place plastic wrap or an old plastic bag under your cookie cutters. This will protect your work surface and make the papier mâché easier to pick up!

Goodie basket

This pretty basket makes a perfect Easter present, especially filled with eggs and cute chicks!

You will need:

- Thin cardstock (letter-sized)
- Ruler
- Pencil
- Scissors
- Felt
- Double-sided tape
- Ribbon
- Markers
- Glue
- Needle and sewing thread
- Stuffing or cotton batting
- Small black beads

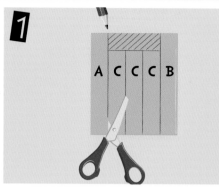

1 From a sheet of cardstock, cut a 1.5 x 11 inch strip from one edge. This is piece A. Next, cut a 1 x 11 inch strip from the other edge. This is piece B. Finally, cut three 2 x 10 inch strips. These are all C pieces.

2 Decorate piece A with markers. Bend it around to make a ring shape and join the ends together with double-sided tape.

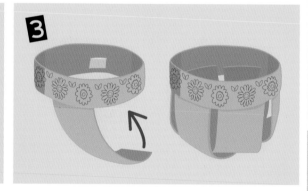

3 Tape the ends of one C piece to the inside of the ring, on opposite sides to make a loop. Add the other two C pieces, spacing them out evenly. There should be a small gap between each piece.

4 Stick the ends of strip B inside the ring to make a handle. Glue ribbon around the outside of the basket to decorate. Make two cardstock flowers and stick one over the join on each end of the handle.

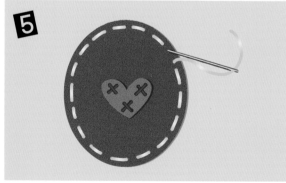

5 Cut two egg shapes and a small heart from felt. Sew the heart to one egg. Place on top of the other egg and sew the two pieces together at the edges. Leave a small gap to add some stuffing, then sew the gap shut.

6

To make a chick, cut out two egg shapes, two wings, and a heart from felt. Sandwich the wings and heart in place between the egg shapes. Sew around the edges and stuff. Glue on black bead eyes and a felt beak.

Tip!
Decorate the handle with ribbon before you attach it to the basket.

Tip!
Fill the basket with crunched-up tissue paper. Rest your chicks and eggs on top so they look extra-cute!

1 2 3

In a spin

These spinning tops are easy to make and "wheely" good fun, too!

Pie, please!

Cut out two circles of cardstock in different colors. Cut one of them into eight equal-sized sections (like a pie). Glue four of the sections onto the other circle so you have alternating colors. Make a hole in the middle, using a sharp pencil. Push the pencil through the hole. Give the wheel a spin, and watch as the colors mix together to make a new shade!

Spot the difference

Cut out another circle, but this time cover it in spots. You can make your own by cutting them from colored paper, or glue on some spotted wrapping paper.

Tip!

The pencil needs to fit quite tightly through the circle. If it feels loose, add some glue to hold it in place.

Loop-the-loop

Make two small holes in the middle of a patterned circle with a needle. Use the needle to push a length of thread in through one hole and back out through the other. Knot the ends together so you have a big loop of thread. To use, hold one end of the loop in each hand, with the circle in the middle. Gently pull in and out to watch the wheel spin.

Tip!

If you don't have any colorful cardstock or wrapping paper, use markers to draw your own patterns onto plain paper.

Dizzy frog

Why not cut out a face instead of a circle? Stick on eyes, a mouth, and some colored spots to decorate. Now, see what happens when you give it a spin!

The cat's whiskers

Draw a cat and cut it out. Add some colorful stripes, a mouth, and a nose. Glue on eyes and ears or see what happens if you cut those parts out instead.

125

Sweet tweets

Grab your crayons and add some dazzling stripes to the animals on these cards.

You will need:

- Thin cardstock (various colors, including white and brown)
- Ruler
- Scissors
- Green felt
- Black marker
- Pencil
- Glue stick
- Crayons

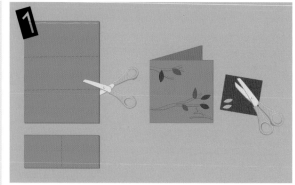

1 Cut a piece of cardstock roughly 3.5 x 8.5 inches and fold it in half. Draw tree branches onto brown cardstock and cut out. Stick the branches to this background. Cut out leaves from green felt and glue to the branches.

TIP! Cut out your animals so the crayon stripes go from top to bottom. They look better this way!

TIP! You should be able to make three cards from a single sheet of letter-sized cardstock.

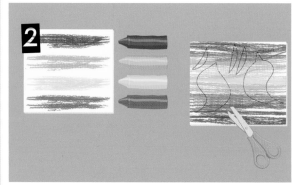

2 Use your crayons to draw bright colors onto plain white cardstock in a striped pattern. Draw two bird shapes on top and cut them out. Cut out wings as well.

3 Use a black marker to draw an eye on both birds. Glue their wings in place. Stick each bird to one of the branches on your card.

TIP!

Make a set of five or six cards with envelopes. Tie them all together with a ribbon to turn your cards into a thoughtful gift.

Go fish!

Draw waves onto the front of a blue card in crayon. Cut out fish instead of birds from your striped patterned cardstock. Draw an eye onto each one and stick to the wavy background.

Gift tags

Make your presents even more special by adding a cool handmade gift tag!

Cutting corners

Cut a rectangle shape out of paper and cut each corner into a nice smooth curve. Stick on scraps of paper and fabric to decorate. Punch a hole at one side and use a narrow strip of paper as a tie.

TIP!

Use felt, colored paper, and googly eyes to make a fun picture on the front of your tag.

Brown paper package tags

Glue some brown paper to a piece of paper. Cut out a label shape and decorate it however you like. Punch a hole at the top. Thread a length of string through the hole to make a tie.

I love photos

Show someone you really love them with a heart-shaped tag. Cut out the heart from paper and punch a hole near the top. Stick on your favorite photograph or cut out a picture from an old magazine instead. Finish off with a ribbon tie or bow.

TIP!

Make sure you ask an adult before you cut up photographs.

Big shape, little shape

Simple shapes, such as circles and triangles, make awesome tags. Decorate them with smaller shapes in different colors. Tie on some nice checked ribbon for the perfect finishing touch.

Make it match!

Make a tag to match the wrapping paper you've used. You can cut out all kinds of different shapes, including butterflies, planes, and teddy bears. To turn them into tags, just punch a hole and thread on a tie. Add some extra decoration with buttons, beads, or sequins.

Funky flowers

Draw and cut out a flower from paper. Glue on a button to make a flower center. Punch a hole in one of the petals and tie on a piece of curling ribbon.

Prints and patterns

Cut a shape from a piece of sponge and dip it in paint. Press onto a piece of paper to make a print. Allow the paint to dry, then cut out a tag around the shape. To make a pattern of circles, try stamping with the end of a pen or pencil instead.

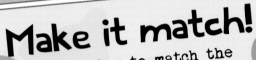

TiP!

Pick a button in a different color so it stands out.

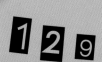
129

Wrap it up

Stencil sheets of festive wrapping paper to finish off your presents with a flourish!

You will need:

- Thin cardboard
- Scissors
- Saucer
- Paper
- Pencil
- Paint
- Kitchen sponges
- Glitter

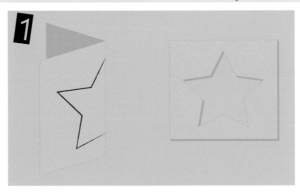

1 Fold a piece of thin cardboard in half and draw half of a star shape against the fold. Cut it out, then open the cardboard out flat again to reveal your star stencil.

2 Pour some paint into a saucer and cut a small piece of kitchen sponge. Place the star stencil in the corner of your paper. Dip the sponge into the paint, then dab it over the stencil. Make sure the whole shape is covered.

3 Keep adding stars in the same way, spacing them out evenly. Leave room in between to paint stars in different colors when the first ones are dry.

4 Sprinkle glitter over some of the stars while the paint is wet. Brush off any extra pieces after the paint dries.

Snowy trees

Draw and cut out a Christmas tree stencil and fill in the trees with green paint. Dip a cotton swab into white paint. Use it to stamp dots of snow in between the trees.

Tip!

Print onto letter-sized paper to wrap small presents. For big ones, use brown parcel wrap, or large sheets of art paper.

Tip!

Stamp with a cotton swab in different paint colors to add decorations to each tree!

Bunch of birds

To make a bird stencil, draw a circle with a tail at one side. Stencil the shape all over your paper. When the paint is dry, stencil a red circle on top of each bird. Draw on a face, wings, and legs with a black marker.

Treasure chest

Pack up your birthday booty in one of these swashbuckling boxes!

You will need:

- Thick cardboard
- Pencil
- Buttons
- White paint
- Kitchen sponge
- Shoebox (or any box with a lid)
- Pencil
- String
- Black paint
- Paintbrush
- Markers

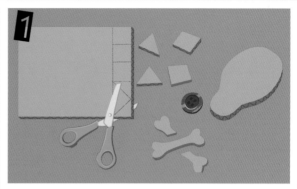

1 Draw a skull and crossbones onto thick cardboard. Cut them out and cut some small squares and triangles from the same cardboard.

2 Glue the skull and crossbones to your box, right in the middle of the lid. Add the other shapes around the edges and along the sides of the box. Stick down some buttons and pieces of string, too.

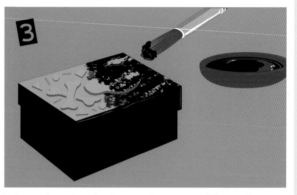

3 When the glue is dry, paint everything (the box and shapes) black. Add a second coat of black paint if you need to. Allow to dry.

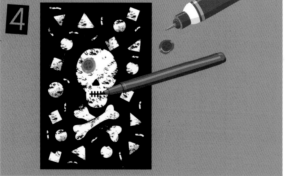

4 Sponge white paint over the stuck-on shapes, so they show up more clearly. Stick brightly colored buttons to the skull as eyes. Draw on a nose and teeth in marker.

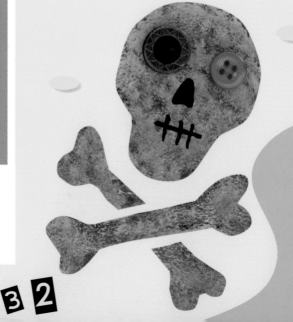

TIP!
Brush the paint on roughly to give your box an old, worn-out look, like a real treasure chest.

TIP!
Make sure you decorate the box with the lid on!

Under the sea

Paint your box blue all over. Cut out fish shapes from cardboard and glue to the box. Add buttons and pieces of string. Sponge on more paint. Finish off by sticking on beads to make gleaming fish eyes.

Bookworm

Give your favorite bookworm a wonderful, wormy bookmark!

You will need:

- Colored paper
- Scissors
- White glue
- Markers or colored pencils
- Pencil
- Googly eyes

TIP!

Add stripes with a gold or silver pen to make a fancy and shiny bookmark.

TIP!

Bookworms can also mark your place in a comic or magazine!

Paper stripes

Stick thin strips of paper across the worm's body instead of drawing them on. Glue them down before you cut out the shape.

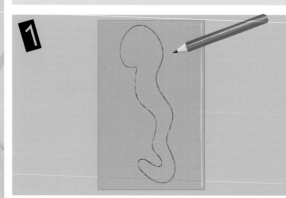

1 Draw the outline of a worm onto a piece of paper, making it as chubby and wiggly as you like.

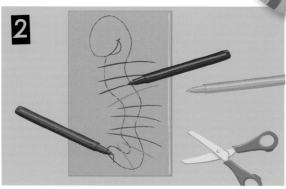

2 Use markers or colored pencils to add multicolored stripes across the body. Cut out, following the outline of the worm.

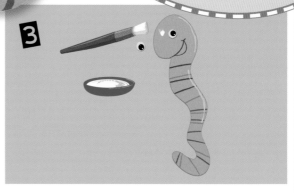

3 Draw on a smiley mouth and finish off by sticking some googly eyes into place above it.

Just for Fun

Birds of a feather

Make a few of these fancy paper birds and hang them all together in a fun flock!

You will need:

- Paper (plain or patterned)
- Cardboard tube
- Double-sided tape
- Colored cardstock
- Yarn or string
- Scissors
- Clear tape
- White glue

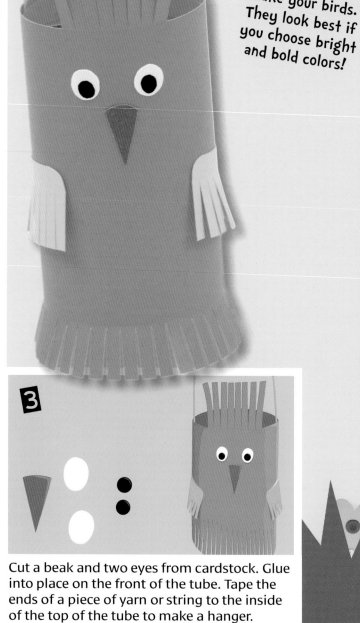

TiP!
You can use plain or patterned paper to make your birds. They look best if you choose bright and bold colors!

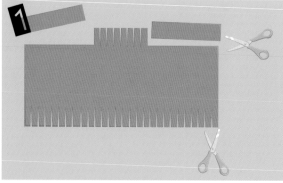

1 Cut a piece of paper long enough to wrap around your cardboard tube. Snip a piece off at each side of the top edge, leaving a small section in the middle. Cut this into a fringe, then cut a fringe along the full bottom edge.

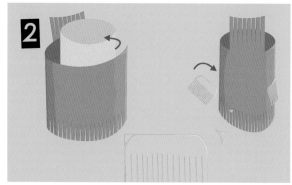

2 Wrap the paper around your tube and stick the ends down with double-sided tape. Cut two rectangles out of cardstock to make wings. Cut a fringe along one edge of each wing and round off the top corners. Stick to the sides of the tube.

3 Cut a beak and two eyes from cardstock. Glue into place on the front of the tube. Tape the ends of a piece of yarn or string to the inside of the top of the tube to make a hanger.

Punky spikes

To give your bird a punky hairstyle, cut spikes into the top part of your paper strip instead of a fringe. Cut some more at the bottom of the strip near to one end to add a spiky tail.

Cute and curly

Draw a curvy, scalloped pattern along the bottom edge of your paper. Cut it out, then stick the paper down. Make a fringe and wings from strips of curling ribbon.

Tip!

Try drawing on eyes with a chunky marker or stick on some googly eyes for a different look.

Fingerprints and flowers

Use dried leaves, flowers, and your own fingers to make a bug-tastic scene!

Fly away home

Dip your finger into red paint and press it down flat near your tree. Try to make a nice, oval-shaped fingerprint. Allow the paint to dry, then use a black marker to turn it into a ladybug, with legs, antennae, and spots.

Start with a tree!

Draw a tree onto brown paper and cut it out. Stick to a plain paper background. Glue dried leaves around the tree branches to decorate.

Blooming marvelous

Cut spiky grass from green paper. Glue along the bottom of the page. Add pressed flowers to some of the stalks. Dip the end of your finger in paint and press gently onto the paper a few times to make tiny fingerprint flowers.

TiP!

To make dried leaves and pressed flowers, pick them from the garden and place onto plain white paper. Place another piece of paper on top, then add a pile of books or a heavy box. Leave for at least a week. Take them out very carefully, as they will now be fragile.

TiP!

To make round fingerprints, use the very tip of your finger. To make oval prints, press the top of your finger flat.

Busy bees

Use yellow paint to make some more oval-shaped fingerprints. Allow to dry. Then add smaller fingerprints in light blue to look like wings. Finish off with black marker eyes and stripes.

Spider pals

Add some black fingerprints, making them round instead of oval. When the paint is dry, draw on eight black legs. Use tiny dots of white paint to make eyes.

Green bugs

Make some green fingerprints. When they're dry, draw legs and details on top with a marker.

TIP!

Dot the white paint on with the end of a toothpick.

Paper faces

Tip!
Try sticking some strands of yarn or thread to the sides of your lion's face to give it whiskers.

Take a plain paper plate and turn it into one of these magnificent masks!

You will need:

- Paper plate
- Paintbrush
- Colored paper
- Pencil
- Paint
- Scissors
- White glue
- Ice pop stick

⚠ Ask an adult for help with this craft.

1 Brush paint all around the edges of your plate. When it's dry, cut the edges of the plate into a wavy pattern.

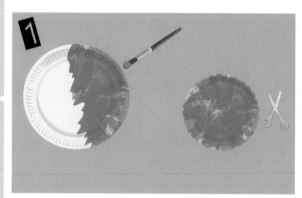

2 Draw a lion's face (with ears) onto a piece of paper and cut it out. Cut extra pieces from paper to make a nose and mouth. Glue them into position, then stick the whole face to the paper plate.

3 Mark two circles for eyes. Use a sharp pencil to make a hole in the middle of each one. Push your scissors through and cut out the eye holes. Glue an ice pop stick to the back, near the bottom, for holding your mask.

Sunflower fun

Decorate a cute sunflower mask by drawing on a smiley mouth and some seeds with a marker.

TiP!

Don't be too neat when you paint the edge of your paper plate. It will look more like a real lion's mane if you let some of the brush marks show!

Paper panda

To turn your paper plate into a panda, cut out two eye patches, a nose, a mouth, and two ears from black paper. Glue into place, then cut out an eye hole in the middle of each eye patch.

⚠ Ask an adult for help with this craft.

TiP!

Use a strip of thick cardboard to make a holder if you don't have an ice pop stick.

Get a-head

1 Cut a strip of black paper long enough to fit around your head, plus a little bit extra for overlapping. Hold it around your head to find the right fit and hold the ends in place. Move it away from your head and tape the ends together.

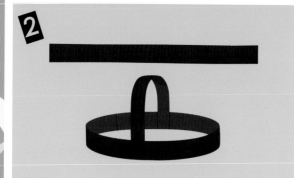

2 Cut another strip of black paper. Put the headband back on your head and ask a friend to mark where your ears are. Take the headband off and stick each end of the strip inside the headband, by each mark.

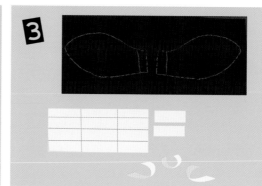

3 Draw a pair of sheep ears onto black cardstock and cut out. Fold over a strip at the narrow end of each one to make a tab. Cut out small strips of white paper. Curl each one around a pencil.

4 Stick the curly paper pieces all over the front of the headband. Glue one ear to each side, with the tab pieces facing backward. Cut out gray cardstock and glue to the inside of the ears for detail.

TIP!

Making paper fit around your own head is tricky! Ask someone to help you out with the first two steps.

Dress-up giraffe

Everyone loves giraffes! Make a plain yellow headband, then decorate it with brown paper spots. Stick on ears and add two paper horns at the top.

Cool kitty

To make a pair of cat ears, fold each one along the middle. Cut the tab in half so you can glue the ears on at an angle.

Finger-puppet fun

Keep all ten of your fingers busy making these cute puppets!

T!P!
Give each of your finger puppets different faces. They could be happy, sad, worried, surprised, giggly, goofy, or even toothy!

Funny face

Wrap a strip of paper about 3 inches tall around your finger. Overlap the edges, then stick in place to make a tiny tube. Cut a pair of arms from paper and glue to the sides. Stick some yarn at the top to make hair. Draw on a mouth in marker and finish off with two googly eyes.

Paper people

Make a finger tube from paper, as before. Cut out a circle of paper and draw a face on one side. Stick it to the top of your tube. Decorate with extra pieces of paper. Use yarn to make hair. Glue buttons or sequins to the tube.

Sheep-shape!

Cut two arch-shaped pieces of white felt, big enough to fit over your finger. Glue or stitch them together, leaving the bottom open. Draw a sheep's head onto felt and cut out. Use a black marker to draw on a face. Glue the head to the top of the body.

T!P!
Stick a photo of a person or an animal to the top of the tube instead of drawing the face.

Puppy love

Make a light brown felt body, gluing or stitching two arches together. Cut out a dog's head, ear, and round snout in the same color. Cut an ear and eye patch from dark brown felt and a nose from black felt. Glue the pieces together, then stick the head to the body and draw a mouth.

Oink!

Cut a pig's head and cute snout from pink felt. Glue them together and draw on a face with a marker. Cut out and stitch a pink felt finger-puppet body. Glue the head and body together.

TiP!

Use face paints to turn your fingers green so they match the dragon's body!

! Ask an adult for help with this craft.

! Ask an adult for help with this craft.

Tiny dragon

Draw the top part of a dragon onto paper and color it in. Cut out, then make two holes near the bottom edge. Push your fingers through the holes to make the dragon's legs. Wiggle them around to make him walk, run, or do something silly, such as dance ballet.

Sir Finger-legs

Draw the head, body, and shield of a knight onto paper. Color it in and cut out. Make holes at the bottom for your fingers, as for the dragon.

Pin on some cheer

Spread some holiday cheer with a colorful Christmassy pin.

You will need:

- Colored cardstock
- Scissors
- Felt
- Markers
- Cotton swabs
- Pencil
- Glue stick
- White paint
- Glitter

1 Draw and cut out a circle of colored cardstock. Cut out a snowman's head from white cardstock. Cut out a hat from a different color and a red cardstock nose. Cut a strip of felt into three pieces for the scarf.

Tip! For a perfect, neat circle, draw around a mug or drinking glass.

2 Stick the head onto the circle of cardstock. Add the hat, nose, and scarf on top. Draw on eyes and a mouth with a marker.

3 To decorate the cardstock around the snowman, add dots of white paint with a cotton swab. Sprinkle glitter on top of some dots while the paint is still wet for some extra snowy sparkle!

Tasty cake

Cut out a Christmas cake and glue to your cardstock circle. Cut two tiny leaves from felt and stick them on top. Add some red beads to look like holly berries.

Red-nosed

Give Rudolph a **very** shiny reindeer nose by gluing on a button. Stick sequins to the pin instead of painting on snowflakes.

How to wear your pin

Fix some double-sided tape onto the back, then stick the badge to your favorite top. Or, if you have got a pin you don't wear anymore, glue your new badge on top!

Transform a T-shirt

Bring old clothes back to life with these cool makeover ideas.
Don't forget to check with an adult before using the tees!

Tip!
Be careful to sew through only the front layer of the T-shirt!

Button face

Draw a circle onto your T-shirt in pencil. Stitch buttons all the way around the circle, mixing up the colors as much as you like. Sew two more in the middle to make eyes. Finish off the face with a stitched smiley mouth.

Tip!
Cut out different shapes, such as hearts or stars, and sew on in the same way. You could even make alphabet letters, to spell out your name or initials!

Join the line!

Fold a paper in three. Draw a small person, extending the arms and legs to each fold. Cut it out (without cutting the folds) and unfold. Trace around the paper onto a piece of felt or fabric. Cut out and pin to your T-shirt. Sew into place with a running stitch.

⚠ Ask an adult for help with this craft.

Something fishy

To make a fish stencil, fold a piece of thin cardboard in half and cut out half a fish shape. Unfold the cardboard for a symmetrical fishy shape. Place the stencil on your T-shirt. Sponge on some fabric paint through the fish-shaped hole. Move it to a different part of the T-shirt and do the same again. Keep going to build up a fun, fishy pattern.

TIP!

Ask an adult to iron the T-shirt before you start painting, and again when the paint is dry.

Butterfly sparkles

Make butterfly stencils, following the fish instructions. Cut out three different sizes and use a mixture of paint colors. Sew on some sparkly beads or sequins to decorate.

Monster madness

Grab a brush and fabric paint. Paint a wiggly shape onto the front of your T-shirt. Sew on two buttons and stitch a zigzag mouth to turn it into a monster.

TIP!

Slip a plastic bag inside the T-shirt when you're using fabric paints to stop your design from leaking through onto the back of the shirt.

149

Cool for caterpillars

Make some fuzzy pom-poms, then turn them into a bunch of fuzzy bugs!

You will need:

- Cardboard
- Scissors
- Large needle
- Felt (black and white)
- Ruler
- Yarn (three colors)
- White glue

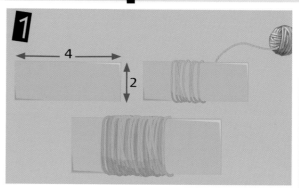

1 Cut a 2 x 4 inch piece of cardboard. Wind your yarn around it widthwise about 40 times. Don't wind too tightly! Snip the end of the yarn strand and carefully slide the whole yarn bundle off the cardboard.

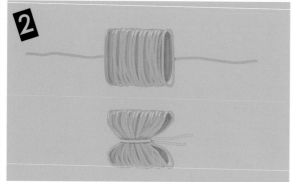

2 Place the bundle down on top of a long piece of yarn. Tie the yarn tightly around the middle of the bundle in a double knot.

3 Cut through the loops on both sides of the bundle to make a pom-pom. Fluff it up with your hands and snip off any straggly ends. Make seven more pom-poms in the same way, using three different colors of yarn.

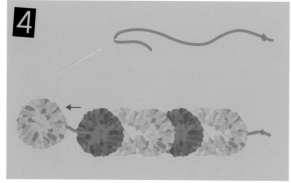

4 Thread a length of yarn onto a needle and knot the end. Push the needle through the tied area in the middle of each pom-pom. Tie a knot to hold the line of pom-poms in place. Snip off the leftover yarn.

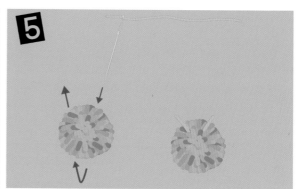

5 To make antennae, sew a piece of yarn down through the head and back up on the other side. Trim the ends so they're the same length. Cut eyes and a mouth from felt. Stick to the head with white glue.

Green and greener

For a multicolored pom-pom, wind two different yarn colors around the cardboard at the same time.

Tip!

Ask a friend to put their finger on the first knot when you're tying the yarn bundle together. It will hold everything in place and make it easier to tie the second part of the knot.

Pom-pom python

Make more pom-poms and thread them together to create a slithery snake. Leave each pom-pom flat instead of fluffing it up so the snake has thinner stripes than the caterpillar. Finish off with a forked tongue cut from felt.

What's the buzz?

It only takes three pom-poms to whip up a busy bee! Sew on two loops of white yarn to look like tiny wings.

Super Splats

Make a mess with your paints, then turn the mess into one of these crazy-cool creatures!

You will need:

- Thin cardboard
- Bubble wrap
- Paper (black and white)
- Markers
- Paint
- Glue stick

1

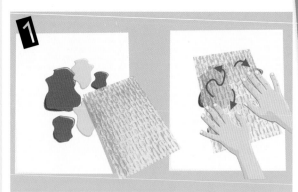

Put four or five drops of colored paint in the middle of a piece of cardboard. Make sure the paint isn't too runny. Place a piece of bubble wrap on top and squish it down with your fingers to mix up the colors.

2

Peel the bubble wrap away and allow the paint to dry. Finger-paint two white dots onto the shape. Add smaller black dots to turn them into eyes. Cut pieces of black and white paper for a mouth. Glue into place.

3

Use colored markers to draw on arms, legs, and any extra things, such as spikes or horns.

Tip!
Sprinkle some glitter onto the wet paint to make a sparkly creature.

Tip!

Use the shape of your splat to help you decide whether your monster needs arms, legs, wings, horns, or any other kind of decoration!

Straw buddies

Grab a straw to make a different kind of splat. Put a few drops of runny paint in the middle of your paper. Hold a drinking straw just above the paper and blow. Point the straw in different directions to make the paint move. Allow to dry, then turn your splat into a monster, as before.

3D Scenes

Find out how to make a plain picture pop with clever 3D tabs.

You will need:

- Letter-sized cardstock (light blue)
- Scissors
- Glue stick
- Paper or thin cardstock, in different colors
- Colored pencils
- Double-sided tape

1

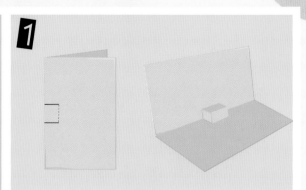

Fold a piece of cardstock in half and press firmly along the crease. Cut two 1.5-inch slits near the middle to make a tab. Fold it over to make a crease. Open the card and push the tab forward so it stands out like a box.

2

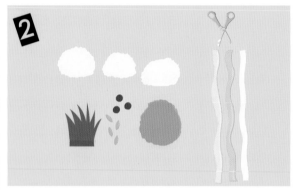

Tear out some white paper cloud shapes. Tear green paper bushes, then cut leaves and colored berries. For the grass, cut spiky shapes and fold over a tab at the bottom edge. Cut wavy strips of paper for the water.

3

Draw a duck onto cardstock and cut out. Color with pencils. Make two ducklings in the same way. Fold two small cardstock rectangles in half to make tabs. Stick one to the back of each duckling, at the bottom.

4

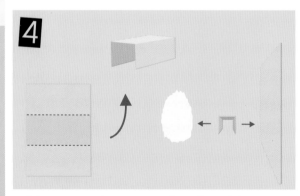

Fold a rectangle cut out of cardstock into three and bend into a "C" shape. Fix double-sided tape to the outside of the two end folds. Stick one side to the back of a cloud and the other to the background cardstock.

5

Fix the pieces in place to build your 3D scene. Add the clouds and bushes first, then the water strips and the grass tabs. Fix the duck to the box tab. Glue the ducklings to the water, using their folded tabs.

Tip!
If you don't have blue cardstock, paint a plain white piece or color it in with pencils.

Tip!
Use another "C"-shaped tab to make one of the bushes stand out like the middle cloud.

Tip!
Fix one grassy section to either side of the box tab, so each sticks out just behind the ducks.

155

Monster mayhem

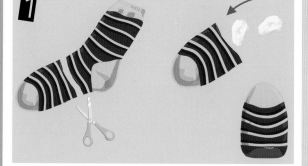

1

Cut off the foot of your sock, just below the heel. Stuff the toe part with cotton balls. Fold over the ends of the sock and glue them together.

2

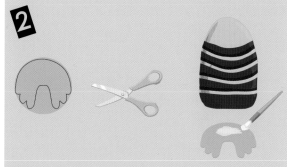

Cut a circle out of cardstock, the same width as your stuffed sock. Cut away the front of the circle to make a pair of feet. Spread glue over the back of the feet. Press the stuffed sock down on top. Allow to dry.

3

Cut eyes, a mouth, and pointy teeth from cardstock. Glue a black pupil to each white eye and stick the teeth on the mouth. Cut arms from the same color as the legs.

4

Stick each cardstock piece to the sock with white glue. If you wish, use masking tape to hold them in place while the glue dries.

Best foot forward

Uh-oh, that sock's escaping! To give your rabbit (or monster) walking feet, cut two oval shapes from cardstock. Stick one under the body to make the normal, flat foot. Stick the other under the body, sticking out enough to fold the front upward at an angle to make the bunny walk!

Funny bunny

To make a sock rabbit, cut the feet, arms, ears, and nose from felt. Glue them on, as before. Add felt or button eyes, some yarn for whiskers, and a cotton ball as a tail!

Tip!

It doesn't matter if your stuffed sock is lumpy—this will just make it look even more monsterlike!

Tip!

For an even crazier look, give your monster giant googly eyes or make one eye bigger than the other! Try cutting feet and hands in different shapes and sizes, too.

Monster measles

Cut circles from brightly colored cardstock and glue them all over your sock to make a spotty monster. Turn him into a Cyclops by sticking on one eye instead of two.

Fancy dress-up

Whether you'd rather be a dashing knight, a fairy princess, or king of the world, you'll love these fun dress-up costumes!

Pretty princess

Tie a 12-inch piece of string between two pencils. Hold the point of one pencil against the center of one edge of a large piece of paper. Stretch out the string and draw a big semicircle with the other pencil. Cut out. Glue curling ribbon to the spot marked by the first pencil. Roll the paper into a cone shape to fit your head. Stick the ends together. Decorate.

Cast a spell

Tightly roll a piece of paper to make a wand handle. Stick some curling ribbon to one end and wind around the handle. Secure at the other end with glue. Cut stars from plain and glittery paper. Stick together, then glue to the top of the wand. Decorate with more ribbon and a heart.

Tip!

Decorate your items with cutout shapes and sparkly sequins or draw on a pretty pattern.

Dazzling tiara

Measure a strip of cardstock long enough to fit around your head and overlap at the ends. Draw the shape of a tiara in the middle, then cut out. Stick the ends of the cardstock together. Decorate!

Fit for a king

Measure a piece of gold cardstock to fit your head. Cut out a triangle with a circle on top. Use this as a pattern to draw the pointed parts of your crown. Cut out the finished crown shape. Decorate with sequins and colored cardstock.

Tip!

If you don't have any gold cardstock, use yellow or orange instead.

Shiny shield

Cut a shield shape from silver cardstock and a slightly bigger one in another color. Glue together. Decorate the middle with colored paper. Cut a strip of cardstock slightly shorter than the width of your shield. Curve the shield round and glue one end of the handle to each side edge on the back of the shield.

Your helmet, sir!

Measure a piece of cardstock to fit around your head. Draw a helmet shape in the middle. Cut out and stick the ends together. For the visor, fold a piece of paper in half. Cut three slits, then unfold and glue into place. Stick a piece of cardstock to the front of the helmet as a nose guard and add feathers at the top to make a plume.

Tip!

No silver cardstock? No problem! Stick some foil to plain cardstock instead.

Get the bug

Are you ready to rustle up some tissue-paper bugs? Bzzzz!

You will need:

- Tissue paper
- Scissors
- Clear tape
- Thin cardstock
- White glue
- Ruler
- Newspaper
- Yarn
- Pencil
- Paper

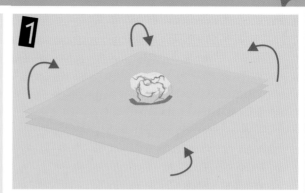

1 Cut three 5-inch squares of tissue paper, all the same color. Roll a sheet of newspaper into a ball. Place it in the middle of the tissue paper. Fold the paper around the ball and tape the edges underneath.

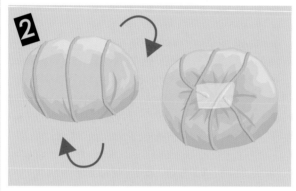

2 Tape a piece of yarn underneath your bug, close to one end. Wrap it around the bug a few times. Tape the other end down to secure.

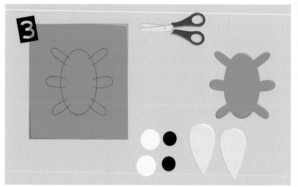

3 Draw an oval shape onto cardstock. Make it slightly smaller than your tissue-paper bug. Add three legs on each side, then cut it out. Cut circles of black and white paper to make eyes and cut out two petal shapes for wings.

4 Spread glue over the middle of the leg section. Press the bug down on top. Stick the wings and eyes into place and allow to dry.

Tip!
Use a tissue bug to decorate a birthday card or invitation.

Tip!
Wrap skinny ribbon around the bug instead of yarn for a cool, shiny effect.

Ladybug, ladybug

Make a ladybug using red tissue paper. Cut out black legs and stick on circles of black paper to decorate.

Glamor bug!

Why not make your bug look pretty? Cover the wings with sparkly sequins and add some button eyes.

Seaweeds

All of these underwater creatures are made from dried and pressed leaves.

Shark attack!

Use a leaf with a jagged or extra piece on one side. This will be your shark's fin. When the leaf is dried, use a small brush to paint on a beady eye and some sharp teeth.

Fishy friends

Stick some small pressed leaves to your paper so they're quite close together. Draw on tails and fins with a marker to turn the leaves into a group of fish.

Tip!

Find out how to press leaves on page 138. It's really easy!

Cutie crabs

Round-shaped leaves with spiky edges make perfect crabs. Draw on some legs and a pair of pincers.

Did you know?
A group of fish is called a shoal.

Turtle-y brilliant!
Add a head and flippers to turn a smooth-edged leaf into a turtle.

Hello, anemone
Draw a simple body and some eyes, then dry fancy or curly leaves to stick on top. You've made an anemone!

Outer space art

Get crafty with crayons and discover how to make waxy space-age patterns. Five, four, three, two, one ... blast off!

1 To make a wax rubbing, place a piece of paper over a rough surface. Rub the side of a crayon over the paper. Brush watery paint all over the colored paper and allow to dry.

2 Draw star trails and circles in different sizes all over the colored paper. Cut them out. Cut small stars and a big circle from yellow paper. Fold the yellow circle into quarters and cut out one quarter section.

Tip! The planets will stand out more clearly against the night sky if you use light-colored paper and crayons.

3 Use black or dark blue paper as your space background. Stick the quarter-circle in one corner to look like the sun. Glue on the circle-shaped planets. Add the yellow stars and some star trails. You could also stick on a rocket or paper rings around some of the planets.

Tip! Look for rough or bumpy surfaces to make your wax rubbings. Try something such as a brick wall, a woven placemat, a cork tile, or a big leaf.

Tip! If your crayon has a paper wrapper, peel it off so you can easily use the side for rubbing.

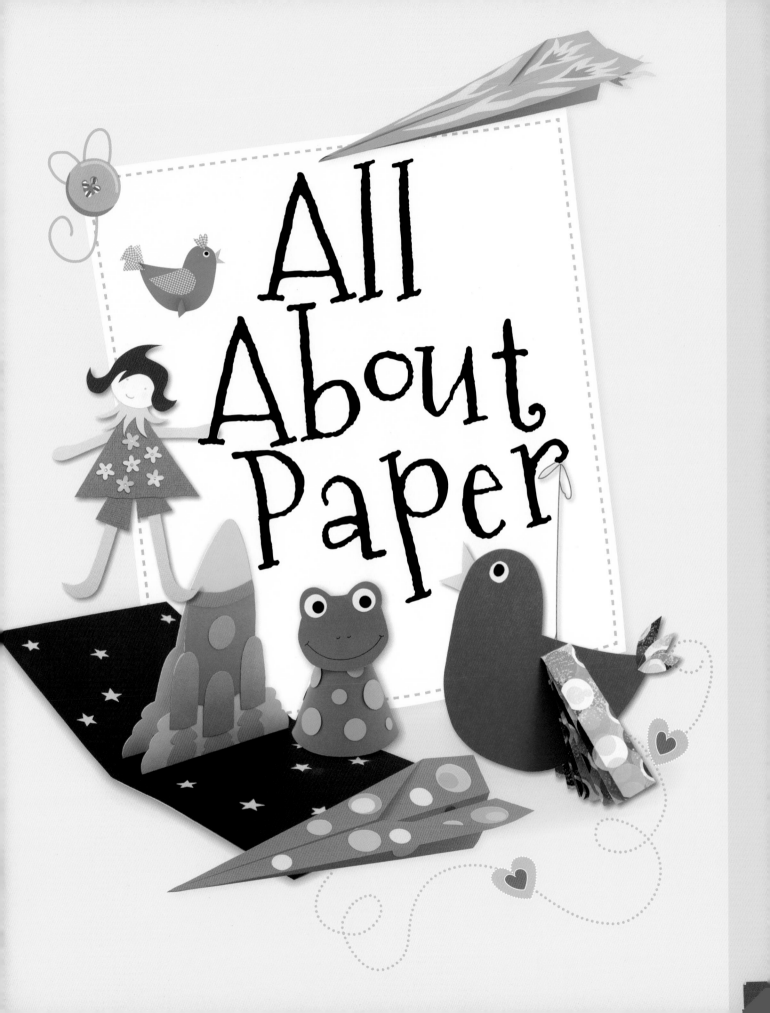

All About Paper

Pop-up mash-up

Simply snip, fold, and stick all these awesome pop-up cards!

You will need:

- Thin cardstock
- Scissors
- Pencil
- Markers
- Paper
- Glue stick
- Sequins (optional)

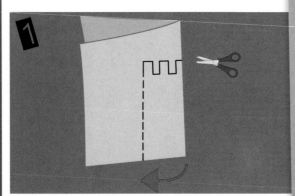

1 Fold a piece of cardstock in half. Just over halfway up the card, cut battlement shapes going in from the folded edge. Open the card and push the tower forward to form a box. Press down on the creases.

2 Glue another piece of cardstock behind the first. Cut two smaller towers from cardstock. Glue one on each side of the box. Cut windows, doors, and branches from black paper and a moon from white paper. Glue into position.

Tip!
Cut out a colored paper flag to fly over your castle.

Tip!
After cutting it out, push the pop-up backward and forward to make a good crease.

Hooting hello

My heart bursts

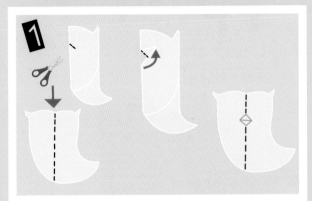

1 Draw an owl shape onto cardstock and cut out. Fold down the middle. To make a beak, cut a small line diagonally upward from the fold. Fold at an angle to crease. Open out the card and push the beak forward.

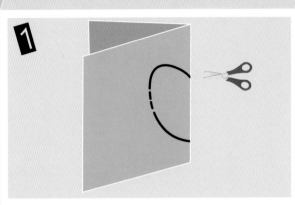

1 Fold your cardstock in two. Draw half a heart against the folded edge. Cut out from both ends, leaving an uncut section in the middle. Decorate, then push the heart forward to make it pop up. Glue to a folded card.

2 Fold a piece of cardstock in half. With the beak pushed forward, stick the owl to the card, lining up the center folds. Draw on feathers. Add a paper wing, legs, and eyes. Cut out leaves and branches. Stick in place.

Tip!

Decorate the card with sequins, paper shapes, and a sparkly silver pen.

Keep on popping

If you can't get enough of pop-ups, here are loads
more ideas to keep your scissors busy!

Snail mail

Start by folding your cardstock
in half. Cut two small slits in
the middle of the folded edge,
roughly 1 inch apart. Fold the
area between the slits backward
and forward to make a crease.
Open the card and push the tab
forward so it makes a box shape.

Stick or draw a garden scene on
one side of the card. Cut out a
snail with a round shell. Use
paint and pieces of a kitchen
sponge to print a pattern on
the shell. Glue the snail to the
front of the box tab.

TIP!

Cut your garden
scene out of an
old magazine.

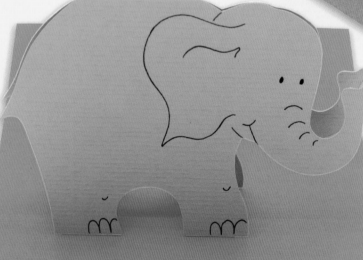

Pack your trunk

Fold your cardstock. Cut two
identical elephant shapes,
making sure they will fit
inside the card. Stick them
together at the top. Place
your elephant's feet at the
card fold and mark where
the feet fall. Make box tabs
for the front and back feet.
Cut each one in half along
the fold line to make four
tabs. Glue one foot to the
outside of each of the tabs
so the elephant stands up.

Pop-it rocket!

Fold your cardstock. Make a box tab as before, then cut the box tab along the fold line so you are left with two rectangular tabs. Cut out two identical rockets and decorate them with colored paper. Stick them together at the top. Glue the bottom edge of the rockets to the outside of each of the tabs. The rocket will stand up when the card is open!

Up, up, and away

Make a box tab as before but stand your card vertically. Decorate the card background with ripped paper clouds and treetops. Draw a hot air balloon and cut it out. Color in with markers. Stick the balloon to the box tab at an angle.

Double pop

Draw a bush on the back of a folded piece of cardstock. Cut two slits, one on either side of the bush shape, into the folded edge. Push scissors through each slit and cut along each side of the bush shape, leaving a section at the top uncut. Push the bush forward and crease along the bottom edge. Crease the card at the top of the bush, too. Close the card, pushing the bush forward to make a final crease. In the bottom folded edge of the bush make a simple box tab for the cow. Cut out a cow from another piece of cardstock and stick in place.

Six little birds

This chirpy bird mobile is flying high!

You will need:

- Thick paper
- Pencil
- Thin cardstock
- Yarn
- Clear tape
- Ruler
- Scissors
- White glue
- Needle
- Aluminum foil

1

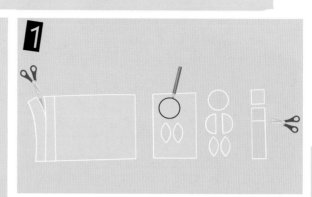

Cut a 1 x 8 inch strip of thick blue paper and a 1 x 1 inch square. Cut a 1-inch square from yellow paper. Draw and cut out a small circle of blue cardstock, then snip it in half. Cut out two blue ovals with pointed ends.

2

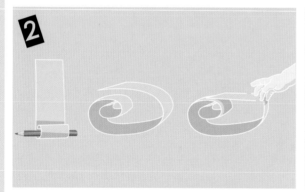

Roll one end of the paper strip around a pencil to make a curl. Curve the strip around and glue the other end above the curl. Pinch the side opposite the curl into a flat point.

3

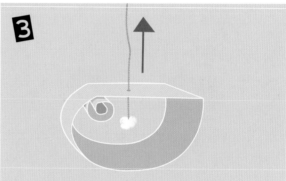

Cut a length of yarn and tie a knot in one end. Use a needle to thread it up through the cardstock shape, just behind the curl. This will be the hanger for your bird.

4

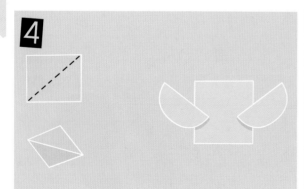

Fold the yellow square in half diagonally so it looks like a beak. Spread glue along the fold and stick to the curved end of the bird shape. Glue the points of the two semicircles to the other square of paper.

5

Stick the square inside the bird so it covers the yarn knot and so the rounded edges of the semicircles face forward. Gently fold them downward to look like wings. Glue the pointed ovals in place to make a tail. Make five more birds like this.

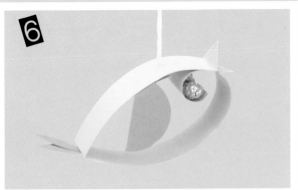

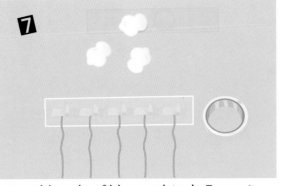

6 To make an eye for each bird, roll a small piece of aluminum foil or black tissue paper into a ball. Dip into some glue, then push into the middle of the paper curl of each bird.

7 Cut a wide strip of blue cardstock. Decorate with white cloud shapes and a smiley sun. Tape the yarn hangers to the back of the strip, spacing them out evenly. Hang your birds at different heights for a more interesting effect.

Fantails and fancy feathers

Thanks to some clever folding, these birds have the coolest wings and tails in town!

You will need:

- Thin cardstock
- Paper
- Ruler
- Clear tape
- Pencil
- Scissors
- Glue stick
- Needle and thread

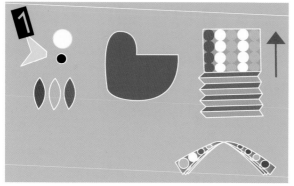

1 Cut a bird shape from cardstock. Cut a beak shape, some circles for eyes, and some tail feathers. Concertina-fold an 8-inch square of patterned paper into 1-inch strips. Bend the bundle of strips in half and crease.

2 Glue the beak, eyes, and tail feathers into place. Cut a diagonal slot just behind the bird's head. Make it a little bit more than 1 inch long, so the wings will fit neatly.

3 Slide the concertina-folded wings into the slot. Pull them gently downward and tape the ends together under the bird's body. Spread the folded wings out to make a fan shape. Add thread to hang the bird up.

Concertina time

You can turn a semicircle into wings, too! Cut and fold into a fan shape. Stick one section to the side of the bird, then open out the rest of the fan.

Tip!

How to concertina-fold:

Fold a 1-inch strip along one edge of your paper. Turn the paper over and make another fold along the same edge. Turn the paper back over and repeat. Keep folding, backward and forward, until you've used up all the paper.

Telling tails

Cut a semicircle out of paper and fold it in half. Fold each half into three equal pieces. Open out and re-fold, like a concertina so the pieces go in and out. Cut a slot in the bird's tail and slide the fan into place.

Smart silhouettes

Make paper silhouettes by mixing bright colors with shadowy black.

Did you know?

A silhouette is a little bit like a shadow. It's a dark, filled-in outline of a shape against a light background. You often see building silhouettes at night, especially in towns and cities.

Skyscraper style

Rectangles make perfect buildings. They can be long and thin or small and wide. Cut them out from orange or yellow paper to make windows, too.

City skyline

Cut out pieces of paper to make this cool city scene. Use black for the building silhouettes and colored pieces on top to look like windows and lights. Square shapes are especially good for windows. Stick them on in groups of four to make separate panes of glass.

Round and round

Colored circles and arches are good for making unusual windows. You could try sticking a black arch or semicircle on top of a rectangle-shaped building, too.

Triangle toppers

Cut triangles of black paper and stick over some of the tall buildings. Add thin lines for aerials or church spires.

Bright blue

Office buildings have loads of windows. Cut long strips of colored paper and stick them down in lines. Use blue instead of orange or yellow for some really sleek city style.

Stained-glass lantern

Cut a long strip of cardstock and carefully cut shapes out of the middle. Stick pieces of colored tissue paper behind the shapes for a stained-glass effect. Curve the cardstock around and glue the ends together. Add a narrow strip of cardstock at the top to make a handle.

⚠ Ask an adult for help with this craft.

Tip!

Hang your lantern in a window so sunlight can shine through the tissue paper.

Haunted house

Make a frame from black cardstock. Draw and cut out a spooky castle and a creepy, spiky tree. Glue them inside the frame. Add some purple tissue paper for the night sky. Use yellow or orange tissue paper behind the doors and windows. Hang the picture in your window and wait for the full moon to make it glow.

Dainty doilies

Snip, snip, snip away to make one of these cool, hole-y decorations!

You will need:

- Colored paper
- Pencil
- Glue
- Yarn or thread
- Clear tape
- Large mug
- Scissors
- Sequins

T!P!
Your decoration will look even better if you cut triangles in a few different sizes!

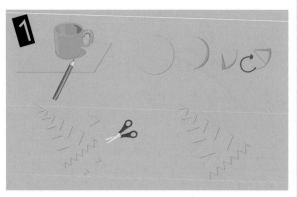

1 Draw around a mug onto paper. Cut out the circle. Fold in half, then in half again. Fold the top part of the quarter-circle in half once more and the bottom part the opposite way. Snip small triangles around the edges.

2 Open out the paper and press the folds flat. Cut out a bigger circle from colored paper. Dot some glue over the back of the cutout shape. Press it onto the colored circle and allow to dry.

3 Stick sequins around the edge and in the middle to decorate. Tape a loop of thread or yarn to the back as a hanger.

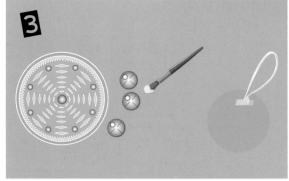

Sparkly square

Fold a square into strips, like a concertina. Snip triangles out of the folds on each side. Open out the shape and decorate with tiny flowers and sequins.

Tip!

Make decorations in different colors and hang them together on a length of string, like a banner.

Diamond in the rough

Start with a square instead of a circle. Fold it in half diagonally, then in half again. Fold the front and back flaps in half, as for the circle. Snip out triangles and unfold the paper. Stick it to the background at an angle, for a diamond.

Flying colors

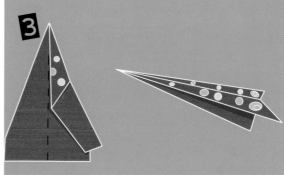

Fold an ordinary piece of paper into one of these plane-ly wonderful flyers!

You will need:

- Letter-sized paper
- Markers to decorate (optional)

TiP!

To add cool stripes to your plane, draw marker lines onto the paper before you start folding. Use as many colors as you like!

1

Fold a piece of paper in half and crease. Open it up again. Fold the top right corner over diagonally so the top edge lines up with the center crease. Do the same with the top left corner.

2

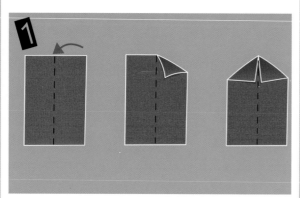

Fold the right-hand side over again. The new corner should meet the center crease. Repeat on the left-hand side. Decorate.

3

Turn the paper over. Fold both outside edges in to the center crease. Turn the paper over again. Push the side edges together. Hold the center fold between your fingers and thumb and open out the sides to become wings.

All fired up

Add some fun flame decorations to make your plane look super slick. Stick them on top of the wings and glue an extra one at the back, in between the center fold.

TIP!

Press firmly along each fold with your fingers to make neat, strong creases.

On the wing

Is it a bird or is it a plane? It's both! Glue on some circles for eyes and two orange triangles as a beak. Add black dots. Snip the back corners of the plane so they look like feathers.

TIP!

Use thin paper to add decorations to your plane and stick the same number of things on each side to balance it out.

Paper shaper

From cats and frogs to witches and wizards, these cute cone characters couldn't be easier to make!

Take bat!

Draw and cut out a semicircle from black cardstock. Move the corners toward each other, so the paper curves around into a cone shape. Overlap the edges and stick together. Cut a head and wings from black cardstock. Draw a face onto the head in silver pen. Glue the head to the top of the cone and the wings to the back.

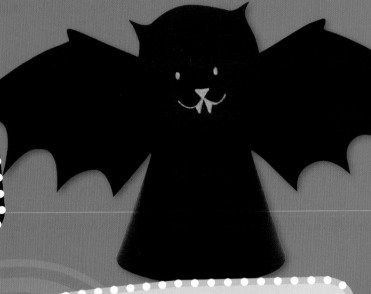

Pretty kitty

Make a black cone, as before. Cut out a head, tail, and white tummy. Cut out an oval-shaped face, with an extra section of fringe on each side to look like whiskers. Stick this to the head and draw on a face. Add a pink triangle to each ear, then glue the head, tail, and tummy pieces to the cone.

Mighty mouse

Tip a brown paper cone sideways and stick a tail to the back. Cut out a pair of ears. Fold over a tab at one end, then glue to the cone and draw on some eyes. Snip white paper into a fringe to make whiskers. Add pink paper to each ear and a pink circle for a nose.

Croak!

Cut out a frog face and stick to the top of a green cone. Add two white circles for eyes. Draw on black pupils, a mouth, and nose. Decorate the cone with circles of light green paper.

Tip!

Use a clothespin to hold your cone together as the glue dries.

Tip!

Decorate the witch and wizard with moons and stars!

Which witch?

Make a black cone, then slide a ring of cardboard over it to look like a hat brim. Draw and cut out a face. Snip a fringe into some white paper to make hair. Glue the face and hair to the cone, underneath the hat brim. Stick arms and hands to the sides of the cone.

Abracadabra!

Make a matching wizard from purple cardstock. Glue an extra piece of paper to the back of the cone as a cloak. Stick a paper beard under the face and stick a thin strip of cardstock to one hand to make a wand.

181

Fairy friends

Cut out some cute paper puppets and finish them off with sparkly sequins!

You will need:

- Thin cardstock
- Pencil
- Sequins
- Clear tape
- Scissors
- Silver pen
- White glue
- Colored pencils

1

Fold a piece of cardstock in half. Draw a wing shape against the fold and cut it out. Cut a circle from cardstock to make a fairy head, a triangle for her dress, two arms, two legs, and some hair.

TIP!

Make your fairy extra magical by using shiny paper for her wings!

2

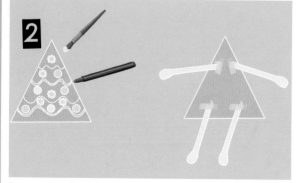

Decorate the dress with a silver pen and glue on some sequins. When the glue is dry, turn the dress over. Tape the arms and legs into place on the back.

3

Stick the dress over the wings. Glue the head to the top of the dress and then add the hair. Use colored pencils to draw on a face. Use sequins or tiny flowers to decorate the hair and shoes.

Ribbon stripes

Decorate a fairy dress with strips of fancy ribbon. Glue them into place and add sequins or silver pen doodles in between.

Elf yourself!

Try making an elf instead of a fairy! Cut out pointy shoes at the end of the legs and make green clothes. Decorate the top with flowers and add a frill around the neck.

Tip!

Tape a loop of thread to the back to turn the elf or fairy into a hanging decoration.

183

Paper mosaic

Make a marvelous mosaic from tiny scraps of paper!

You will need:

- Colored paper
- Scissors
- Glue stick
- Pencil

1

To make the background, take a piece of light blue paper. Cut some green paper into a curved shape. Stick it to the bottom of the blue piece so it looks like a hill.

2

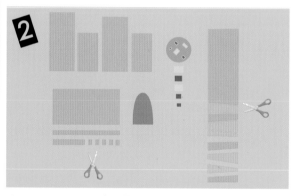

Cut out rectangles from gray paper to make the castle. Cut tiny squares and strips from a lighter gray. Cut out circles for the trees, plus smaller pieces to stick on top. Cut out strips to make a path.

3

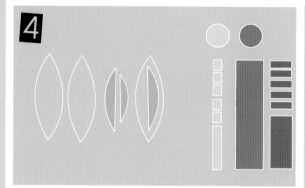

Stick the tiny squares and strips to the castle. Glue the castle to the top of the hill. Add the trees and path. Cut out a sun and some orange rays. Make wispy clouds by gluing pieces of white paper in wavy lines.

4

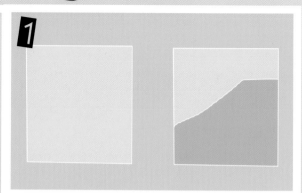

Draw and cut out some green leaves. Cut out circles to make flowers. Add small squares around the edges for petals. Glue to the bottom of the hill.

Did you know?

A mosaic is a picture made from loads of tiny colored pieces. The Ancient Romans used stone tiles to make their mosaics, but paper is easier and looks just as good!

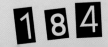

Tip!

Finish off the castle with a cool door and narrow windows. Add a fluttering flag to the highest tower!

Tip!

Your mosaic pieces can be squares, strips, or rectangles. Don't worry about making them look too neat or perfect.

Deck the halls

Get ready for Christmas with some gorgeous ornaments and dangly decorations!

Let it snow

Fold and cut out a circle from white or blue paper, using the instructions on page 176. Cut cool snowflake patterns. Stick your snowflake to some silver paper so it sparkles! Use thread to hang up.

Have a ball!

Cut out six identical circles and fold them in half. Stick the right side of the first circle to the left side of the second. Then, stick the right side of the second circle to the left side of the third. Repeat, until you've joined all six together. Add a loop of ribbon for hanging. Try using different types of paper and vary them for interest.

Tip!

Make a star or bell-shaped decoration in the same way.

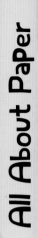

Ring, ring

Cut green, red, and white paper into strips. Curve one strip around into a ring and glue the ends together. Repeat with a second strip. Stick it over the first one, at an angle. Keep adding strips until you have a ball shape. Stick a paper loop at the top for hanging.

Lovely lantern

Fold a rectangle of paper in half lengthwise. Cut slits from the fold toward the opposite edge, leaving about 1 inch at the end uncut. Unfold the paper. Curve the short ends around and stick together. Stick a strip of paper to the top of the lantern as a handle.

Chain reaction

Concertina-fold a sheet of paper and draw a shape on the top fold. Leave a strip at the top and bottom and make sure part of the shape overlaps the folded edges. Cut out, then unfold the paper and decorate.

TIP!

The waste-paper circles from a hole punch are perfect for decorating little Christmas trees!

It's a snap

Have fun decorating your own pack of cards, then deal them out and get playing!

You will need:

- Thin cardboard
- Ruler
- Paint
- Carrot
- Markers
- Pencil
- Scissors
- Saucer
- Small knife

! Ask an adult for help with this craft.

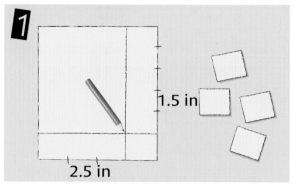

1

Make pencil marks 2.5 inches apart along the top and bottom of a piece of cardboard. Join the dots with a ruler. Draw marks 1.5 inches apart along the sides. Join those, too, to make rectangles. Cut out. Repeat and cut out 12 more rectangles for 36 in total.

2

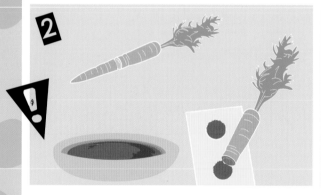

Put some paint in a saucer. Carefully cut the end off a carrot and dip the flat part into the paint. Press onto your cards to make dots. Print three of each number of dots, from one to six, in two different colors.

3

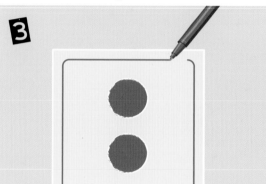

When the paint is dry, draw a border around each card to finish it off. Use colorful markers.

How to play

Snap (for up to 3 players)

- Put all the cards on the table, face down. Shuffle them around, then collect into a pile. Deal the same number of cards to each player.
- Take turns placing a card face up on the table. If two cards with the same number of dots are placed down one after the other, the first person to say SNAP wins the pile.
- Keep playing until one player has collected all the cards.

Pairs

- Spread the cards out, face down.
- Each player turns over two cards for everyone to see. If they match, the player keeps the cards and gets another turn. If they don't match, the player turns them face down again, and the next person has a turn.
- Keep playing, taking turns, until all the cards have been matched into pairs. The player with the most cards at the end wins.

⚠ Ask an adult for help with this craft.

Tip!

Round off the corners of each card with scissors. This will stop them from getting bent and worn out as you use them!

Tip!

Not sure how many dots to print? Use this easy chart to help out.

print **3** cards with **1** dot
print **3** cards with **2** dots
print **3** cards with **3** dots
print **3** cards with **4** dots
print **3** cards with **5** dots
print **3** cards with **6** dots

Then, change paint colors and do it all over again!

Tip!

When you play Pairs, watch the cards and try to remember where they are!

Say cheese!

Try drawing smiley faces onto your cards instead of printing dots.

Tip!

To make it trickier, add an extra rule! As well as matching the number of dots, try matching the color and shape, too.

Mix and match

Cut off the sides of the carrot to make a diamond stamp. Print one set of the above with dots and one set with diamonds for even more fun!

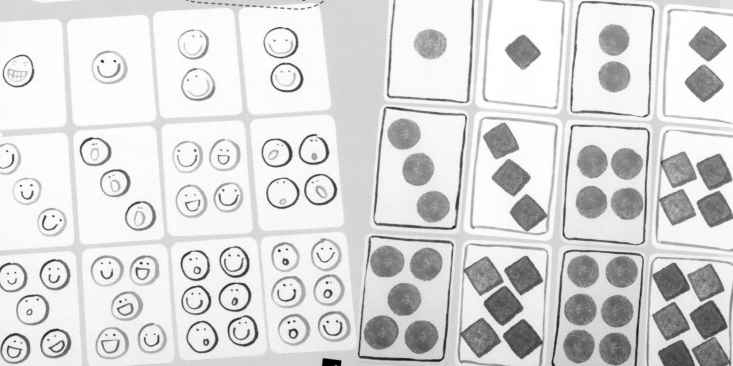

Snake charmer

Use some simple origami to turn a square of paper into a sssuper ssslithery sssnake!

You will need:

- Paper (e.g. leftover gift wrap)
- Double-sided tape
- Markers
- Scissors
- White glue

1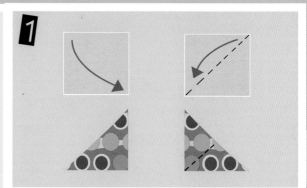

Place a square of paper patterned side down. Fold in half diagonally. Open up, then fold in the opposite direction. Unfold it again. The creases should make an "X" across the square.

2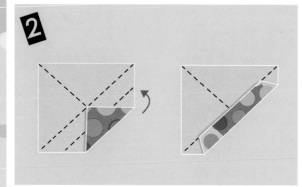

Fold one corner in to the center. Then fold the edge over to meet the center, too. Turn the paper around and do the same on the other side. Open up the paper so the patterned side is facing down.

3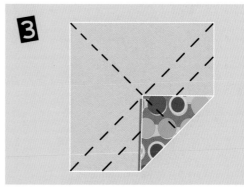

Use the creases you've already made to fold over a triangle at one side, reaching the point to the center crease.

4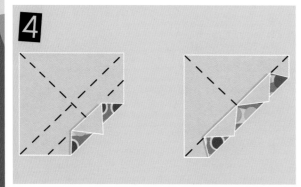

Fold the same triangle back on itself along the next crease. Flip the paper over. Fold the last strip up along the crease. Turn the paper around, flip it over so it's patterned side down, and do steps 3 and 4 again.

5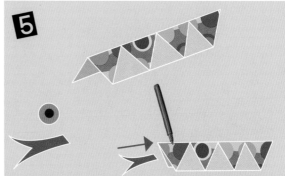

Stick the triangles down. Fold the paper along the center crease, patterned side out. Your snake can now stand up! Cut out two eyes and glue in place. Add black dots. Cut out a forked tongue and glue into place.

Tip!

Press firmly along each fold to make nice sharp creases.

Did you know?

Origami is a special type of paper folding that comes from Japan. It can be used to make all kinds of amazing shapes and models, including snakes!

Sequin scales

Stick shiny sequins along the back of your snake for a cool, scaly look!

Fake snake

If you don't have any wrapping paper, don't worry! Use a plain sheet of paper and decorate it on one side using a marker. Try drawing spots, stripes, stars, or even a snakeskin pattern!

Paper-chain party

These paper chains are easy to make and loads of fun to decorate!

Folded flowers

Concertina-fold a long strip of paper. Draw a flower on top. Make sure the petals on each side go right up to the folded edges. Cut out, snipping through all the layers of paper, but not through the fold itself. Unfold the chain. Stick a circle of yellow paper in the middle of each flower.

Fishing for fun

Cut a chain of fish from concertina-folded colored paper. Use a hole punch to give each one a beady eye. Draw on fins, tails, and smiley mouths.

Simple stars

Concertina-fold shiny or patterned wrapping paper to cut out a chain of star shapes.

TIP!

If you need help with concertina folding, turn to page 173!

TIP!

Add glue and sprinkle on some glitter to make your stars even more sparkly!

Little brown houses

Concertina-fold a strip of brown paper. Draw a house on the top layer. Make sure the roof edges go right up to the folds. Cut out and unfold. Cut squares from an old newspaper or magazine. Glue one to each house as a window.

Tip!

Don't fold your paper too many times. The more layers there are, the harder it will be to cut out your shape!

Snake eyes

Fold a strip of paper, as before. Draw a snake on top, with its head against one folded edge and its tail against the other. Cut out and unfold. Glue strips and triangles of colored paper along the snake's body. Add eyes using a hole punch or marker.

Lovebirds

Make your concertina folds quite wide and draw a bird on the top one. The head and beak should go right up to one folded edge and the tail up to the other. When you unfold the chain, some of the birds will be kissing beaks!

Make a stand

Say hello to their royal highnesses, the King and Queen of fancy paper!

You will need:

- Thick paper
- Pencil
- Double-sided tape
- Gold cardstock
- Beads or sequins
- Narrow ribbon (optional)
- Ruler
- Scissors
- Patterned paper
- Marker

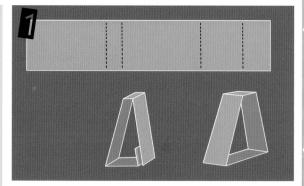

1 Cut a 2 x 11 inch strip of thick paper. Draw a line 4 inches from one end. Add more lines 5, 8, and 10 inches from the same end. Fold along each line to make a 3D stand. Glue the ends together.

2 Cut out a cloak shape big enough to cover the 3D stand. Cut out some sleeves, two hands, and a face. Draw on eyes, a nose, and a mouth. Cut out a crown and stick on some beads or sequins.

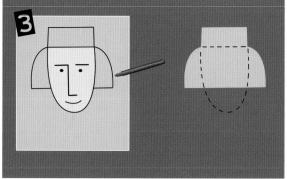

3 Place the face on a piece of cardstock. Draw a hairstyle around the sides and an extra piece at the top. Take the face away and add a line across the bottom of the hair. Cut out the whole shape.

4 Glue the crown to the top of the hair and add the face below. Stick a hand to the back of each sleeve, then glue the sleeves to the cloak. Stick the cloak to the front of the stand. Decorate with shiny paper, ribbon, and sequins.

Tip!

Every king needs a queen! Make one to match, using the same instructions.

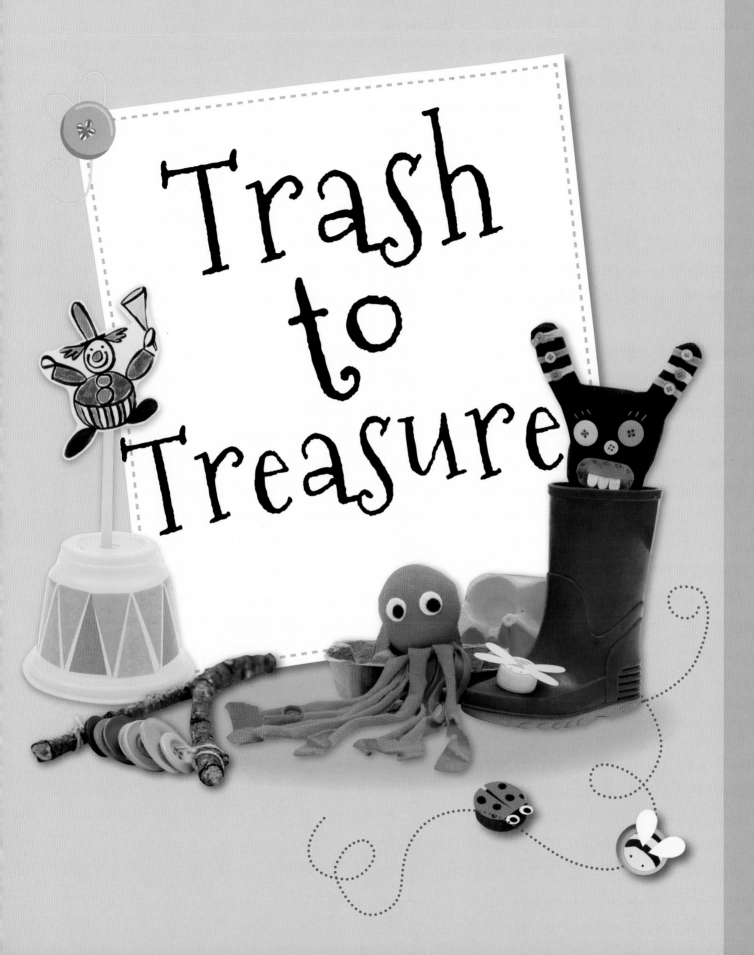

Trash to Treasure

Junk to jungle

Create a cool collage from scrap paper and old magazine pages.

You will need:

- Colored paper
- Scissors
- Markers
- Old magazines and catalogs
- Pencil
- Glue stick

1 Trace or draw animal and bird shapes onto colored paper and cut them out. Cut out extra details, such as beaks and ears, from old magazines or catalogs. Pick pages with interesting patterns and designs.

2 Cut out some big tropical leaf shapes. Use a mixture of colored paper and old magazines. Pictures of plants, leaves, or flowers are especially good for patterns!

3 Pick a plain piece of colored paper to use as your background. Stick a piece of green paper on top as grass. Stick the animals and birds into place. Glue plants and leaves around the edges to make a leafy jungle.

Tip!
Always ask an adult before you start cutting up magazines.

Tip!
Add extra details to your collage with markers. You could draw branches, water, insects, and faces for your animals.

Tip!
Try cutting out different types of animals to make a woodland picture or an underwater scene instead!

Tip!
Make sure you can still see the animals when you stick your leaves into place. It looks great if they're peeping out from behind them!

197

Santa cushion

Turn an old shirt into a fun cushion shaped like Santa's head!

You will need:

- An old light-colored shirt (ask an adult first)
- Needle and thread
- Scissors
- Stuffing
- Fabric
- White glue
- Felt (red, white, pink, and black)

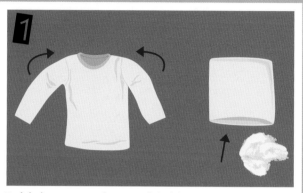

1 Fold the arms of your old shirt to the back and sew together. Sew the top of the shirt together across the neck. Fill the body with stuffing so it looks like a padded cushion. Sew the bottom edges together.

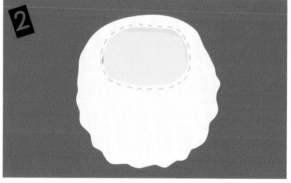

2 Cut out an oval shape from felt, big enough to cover the cushion. Cut a hole near the top for Santa's face. Sew around the edges of the face to join the felt to the cushion. Cut wavy edges for a beard.

3 Cut out felt eyes, cheeks, a mouth, two mustache pieces, and eyebrows. Cut two red felt triangles to make a hat. Sew the sides together with a running stitch. Cut a strip of white felt to fit along the bottom.

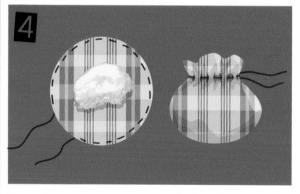

4 To make pom-poms, cut a circle of fabric. Sew running stitches around the edge. Put some stuffing in the middle of the circle. Pull the thread ends to gather the fabric around the stuffing. Knot to secure.

5 Stick one pom-pom to the hat. Use another as Santa's nose. Glue on the other face pieces and add the hat to the head. Sew the white felt strip along the bottom of the hat, stitching through the cushion, too.

Tip!

Ask a grown-up to help you iron the shirt and felt before you start sewing.

Tip!

If you don't have any stuffing at home, cut more old clothes into small pieces and use them to fill your cushion. You could use old tights or socks, too.

Tip!

Sew the bottom strip of the hat into place with cross stitches. They'll hold the layers of fabric together and decorate the felt, too!

The odd-sock zoo

Recycle your old socks and tights to make a zoo full of crazy creatures!

Sock snakes

Take a long sock or one leg from a pair of tights and stuff with cotton batting. Tie the end shut. Cut a forked tongue from felt and sew on buttons for eyes.

Tip!

You can use yarn, thread, curling ribbon, or a rubber band to tie up the end of your snake.

Top caterpillar

Make a long, stuffed body following the snake instructions. Tie thread or rubber bands around the body to make six small sections. Thread two pieces of yarn through the middle of each section as legs. Knot on either side to hold in place. Sew on two buttons for eyes.

Itsy Bitsy

Fill the toe section of a sock with cotton batting. Wrap a rubber band underneath to hold the stuffing inside. Cut the rest of the sock into eight equal pieces. Sew or glue them against the sides of the body to make spider legs. Stick on some googly eyes and tie thread to the top as a hanger.

Tip!

Striped socks are especially good for making lizards, snakes, and caterpillars!

We're off to see the lizard

Cut one leg from a pair of old tights. Stuff with cotton batting and tie the end shut. Cut four feet from green felt. Glue into place. Sew on two buttons for eyes. Add stitches in a zigzag pattern to make a mouth.

Octo-pal

Stuff the toe of a sock, following the spider instructions. Cut the bottom section into eight pieces to make legs. Glue a circle of cardboard just below the body so the legs hang down evenly. Cut two felt eyes and glue into place.

Beady-eyed bird

Turn mismatched socks into cute hand puppets. To make a bird, stick craft feathers near the top of the head. Cut two circles of felt. Add a bead on top of each one and glue or stick to the bird as eyes.

Spiky lizard

Sew through and knot pieces of yarn all the way along the top of the head to make a cool lizard. Sew on a pair of button eyes. Cut out a felt tongue and stick it inside the mouth part of your sock.

Fish foot!

For a fun fish puppet, cut out some felt fins. Glue to the top and sides of the sock. Add a piece of pink felt inside the mouth section and stick on two button eyes.

Picture patchwork

Stick scraps of fabric and felt together to make this colorful countryside picture.

You will need:

- Scrap paper
- Fabric
- Marker
- White glue
- Pencil
- Scissors
- Felt

1 Draw a background of hills and fields onto scrap paper. Cut out the shapes to use as patterns. Place each shape on a different piece of fabric. Trace around the outside in marker and cut out.

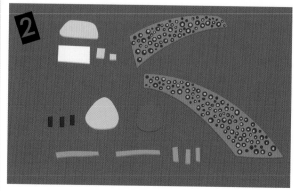

2 Cut out simple shapes from felt to make trees and houses. Cut some curved shapes for roads and long, thin strips for fences.

3 Draw and cut out some flowers and butterflies. Lastly, cut out a strip of spiky grass to fit along the front of your countryside scene.

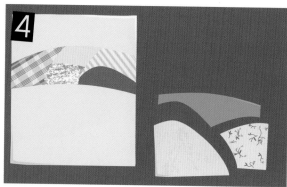

4 Use a piece of blue paper to make your background. Stick the fabric fields and hills into place, fitting them back together like a jigsaw. Glue the trees, houses, roads, and smaller details on top to decorate.

Tip! The picture you make doesn't have to be the same as this one! Use it to give you ideas, then make up your own design.

Tip! Your background paper needs to be the same size as the scrap paper you cut up to make the patterns at the start. Letter-sized sheets are perfect!

Tip!
Snip pieces of fabric from old clothes. It's cheaper than buying pieces of material in a store and planet-friendly, too!

203

Glove love

1

Turn your glove inside out. Cut off the thumb and two middle fingers. Sew the holes shut. Then turn the glove the right way out again.

2

Fill the glove with stuffing or cotton batting. Sew over the end to hold the stuffing inside.

3

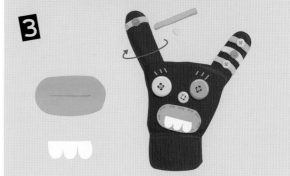

Cut out a felt mouth and teeth. Sew to the front of the glove. Stitch on buttons to make the eyes and nose. Wrap strips of felt around the horns. Sew a button over the join in each strip. Make stitches for eyebrows.

Glove bunny

To make a rabbit, cut off the thumb and two smallest fingers. Sew the holes shut, as before. Stuff the fingers and stitch to the sides of the glove to make arms. Cut paws from felt and sew into place. Stuff the glove and tie closed with yarn. Sew on buttons for eyes and a nose and tie a yarn bow to one ear as a cute decoration.

Silly side

Make the side view of a funny friend from a fingerless glove, using the thumb as a nose. Sew the open finger and thumb ends together. Sew a button on the thumb. Sew one eye and a mouth on the same side as the thumb. Sew and tie strips of yarn along the top edge to make spiky hair.

205

Pocket pouch

Cut neatly around the stitched edges of pockets from your old clothes and turn the pockets into smart pouches or change purses!

Zippy face

Zippers on pockets make perfect mouths. Sew two buttons above the zipper to give your pocket a fun face. Glue on circles of felt to decorate.

Tip!

Be careful to sew through only the front piece of the pocket so you don't sew the pouch closed!

Wrist action

Decorate a plain pocket with a felt flower. Sew it into place with a button in the center. Fold a loop of ribbon big enough to slide over your hand. Stitch the ends to one side of the pocket. Slip the loop over your wrist to carry the change purse.

Handy handbag

Cut a piece of felt the same width as your pocket and 4-5 inches tall. Snip the top and bottom edges into a "V" shape. Glue to the bottom of the pocket. Snip the ends of the felt into a fringe, and stick a row of sequins along the top. Cut a long piece of ribbon to make a shoulder strap. Glue or sew the ends to the back of the pocket.

Toothy grin

Find a pocket with two buttons near the top. Cut a mouth and some teeth from felt. Glue to the front of the pocket, underneath the button eyes. Cut an extra strip of felt, an inch or so shorter than the height of your pocket. Glue the ends of the strip to the back of the pocket to make a belt loop.

Add your own eyes to a pocket by stitching on a pair of buttons!

Pocket peepers

Choose a pocket that has a fold-over flap at the top. Glue or sew two buttons at the top to look like eyes.

Growing green

Use household trash to turn your yard into a plant paradise!

Did you know?

The official name for a mini-greenhouse like this is a "cloche."

Green-y in a bottle

Turn an old plastic bottle into a mini-greenhouse for your garden. Wash the bottle and peel off the label. Carefully cut off the bottom end with sharp scissors. Plant your seeds in the garden and place the bottle on top. Push it gently down into the ground. The bottle will keep the seeds safe and warm as they grow.

! Ask an adult for help with this craft.

Tip!

You can easily lift up the bottle to water your seeds. On warm or sunny days, you can also take the lid off so your seedlings get some air!

Egg-plants!

Fill each section of a cardboard egg carton with some soil or compost. Plant seeds in the soil, following the instructions on the packet. When your seedlings have grown enough to move out into the garden, you don't need to lift them out of the box. Just plant the whole biodegradable egg carton in the ground!

Tip!

If you want to plant the seedlings in different parts of the yard, just snip off individual sections of the egg carton.

Flower boots

Take a pair of old rubber boots and drop some medium-sized stones or pebbles into the bottom. Then, fill the rest of the boots with soil. Plant vegetables, herbs, or pretty flowers in the soil and watch them grow.

Tip!

The stones and pebbles will stop the soil in your boots from getting too soggy. Plants love water but not too much of it!

Tip!

You can plant paper pots right in the ground, just like the egg cartons.

Paper pots

Wrap a strip of newspaper or brown paper around a jelly jar a few times. Take the jelly jar away. Fold over the top edge of the paper to hold the wrapped shape in place. Tuck the rest of the paper in at the bottom. Fill your paper pot with soil and add some seeds.

Sprout hair

Cut a piece of paper big enough to wrap around a jelly jar. Draw a funny face or a monster on the front. Fill the jar with cotton batting, then sprinkle alfalfa seeds or beansprout beans on top. Wrap the paper around the jar and stick the ends together. Water the seeds or sprouts and watch as your monster grows hair!

Tip!

Instead of wrapping paper around the whole jar, just glue on a face. Then, you can watch through the glass as the roots grow, too. Remember to remove the label first.

Farmyard friends

Tear up old brown envelopes and yesterday's newspapers to make these feathery farmyard birds.

You will need:

- Colored paper
- Scissors
- Marker
- Old brown envelope
- Old newspaper
- Pencil
- Glue stick

Tip!

You can recycle white envelopes as well as brown ones. Loads of them have really cool patterns printed on the inside. Tear one open and see what you find!

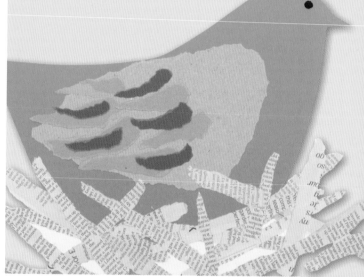

1

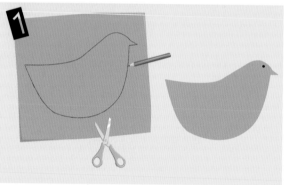

Draw a hen onto paper and cut her out. Add an eye using a black marker.

2

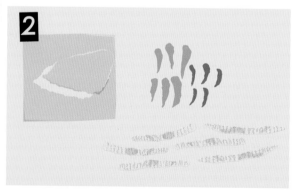

Tear a wing shape from an old brown envelope. Tear smaller strips of brown paper to make feathers and small strips of newspaper for straw.

3

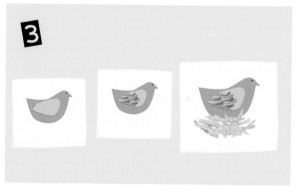

Stick the hen onto a white paper background. Glue the wing and feathers on top. Add the strips of newspaper to make her nest.

Owl mail

Cut an oval shape from brown paper. Tear out wings, feet, feathers, and a face. Glue them to the oval to make a fluffy but wise old owl.

Cock-a-doodle-doo!

Cut and tear paper pieces to make a rooster. Add a comb to his head and a big, feathery tail.

Bottle-top bugs

Start saving up your bottle tops so you can make these fun bugs!

You will need:

- Red or black bottle top
- Paper (red and black)
- Pencil
- White glue
- Glue stick
- Marker
- Glue spreader
- Scissors

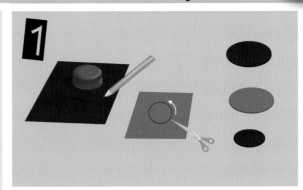

1 Draw around your bottle top onto black paper and again onto red paper. Cut out both pieces. Cut a smaller circle of black paper for the head.

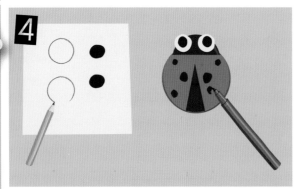

2 Stick the black circle onto the top. Glue the head on top so it overlaps the edge a little bit.

3 Snip a small piece off one side of the red circle. Cut out a triangle on the opposite side to make the wings. Spread glue along the flat edge of the wings. Stick to the top, just behind the head.

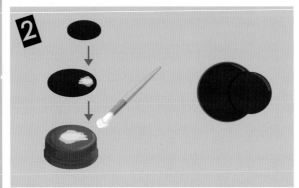

4 Cut out two circles of white paper and two smaller black circles. Stick together to make eyes, then glue to the front of the head. Use a marker to draw black dots on the wings.

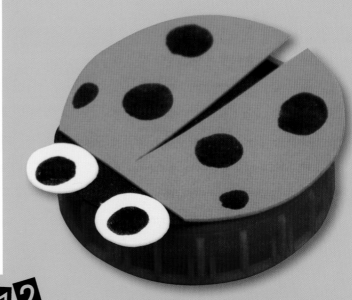

TIP!
If you can't find tops in the right color for your bugs, try painting a plain white one the color you want instead.

TIP!
Bend the wings up a little bit at the back. It will make your ladybug look like it's about to fly away home!

Bottle-top bumblebee
Draw marker stripes onto yellow paper to make a cute bumblebee. Cut petal shapes from white paper to make wings and add small black dots for eyes.

Dragonflies
Make double wings by cutting out four long petals. Use shiny paper for an even prettier bug!

Meet the beetles
To give your bug a slick, patterned body like these beetles, stick a circle of striped paper to the top. Snip two circles in half to make two sets of wings and add a smaller semicircle on top for the head. Use sequins for eyes.

Making music

Have fun making these cool musical instruments.
Then get noisy and try playing them!

Guitar hero

Cut 1-inch slits around the end of a cardboard tube. Bend the pieces back and stick them to the side of an old tissue box. Paint the tube and the outside of the tissue box. Carefully stretch rubber bands around the box to make guitar strings.

TO PLAY: Strum and pluck the strings.

Tip!

Decorate the front of your guitar with a painted pattern or stencil. This one has flowers made from finger and thumb prints!

Rainmaker

Glue small, tightly rolled balls of foil randomly to the inside of a cardboard tube, as far inside as you can get them. Cut a circle of cardboard a little bit bigger than the end of the tube. Snip around the edges to make a fringe. Glue the fringe inside the end of the tube so the circle fits nicely at the end. Drop in some dry beans or lentils. Stick another fringed circle in the other end of the tube to hold the beans inside. Decorate the outside of your rainmaker with paper and ribbon.

TO PLAY: Tip from side to side so the beans fall through the tube, making the sound of rain.

Shaker maker

Paint and decorate the bottoms of two paper plates. Pour dried beans or lentils onto one of them. Glue the plates together at the edges to seal the beans inside. When the glue is dry, your shaker is ready to shake!

TO PLAY: Shake like a tambourine.

Honk your horn!

Decorate a long cardboard tube (the kind you find inside a roll of wrapping paper is good). Use a sharp pencil to make a row of eight holes on one side. Cut a circle of waxed paper, wider than the tube. Wrap it around the bottom end and hold in place with a rubber band.

TO PLAY: Blow into the open end. Cover the holes with your fingers to make different notes.

⚠ Ask an adult for help with this craft.

Full of beans

To make a different kind of shaker, fill a glass jar with beans, leaving a little space at the top. Put the lid on and your shaker is ready to use! Add some strips of paper or shiny stickers if you want to decorate the jar.

TO PLAY: Shake in all directions, fast or slow.

Button shaker

Find a "Y"-shaped stick. Thread some buttons onto a piece of string. Tie one end of the string to each side of the "Y", pulling the string tight. Snip off the thread ends to finish.

TO PLAY: Hold the handle and shake from side to side.

Sew Christmassy

These Christmas decorations are soft, festive, and just a little shiny, too!

You will need:

- Felt
- Stuffing
- Small beads
- Needle and thread
- Scissors
- Sequins
- Button
- Pins

Tip! Try using cotton batting if you don't have any stuffing.

1

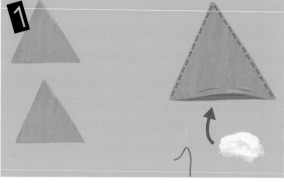

Cut out two identical triangle shapes from green felt and pin them together. Sew them together around two of the sides, using a running stitch. Push some stuffing inside, then sew the third side shut.

2

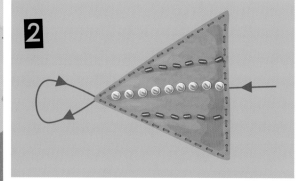

Sew a line of stitches down the middle of the triangle. Sew through both layers of felt and the stuffing. Add a sequin and bead to each stitch as you go. Sew two more lines on either side, adding small beads as you go.

3

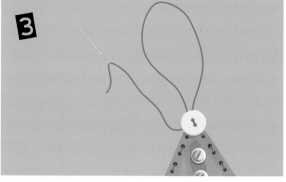

Stitch a button to the top of the felt tree. Add a loop of thread to make a hanger. Now hang your decoration on the tree or in the house!

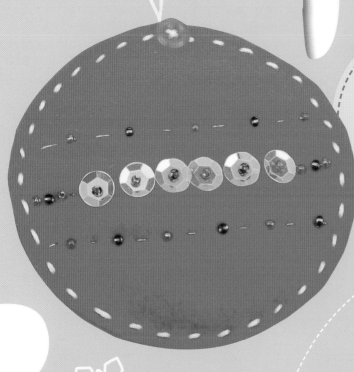

Going round

Cut out circles from felt to make a round ornament shape. Sew together and stuff, as before. Sew a line of beads and sequins or a strip of ribbon across the center. Decorate with lines of stitches or a number of sparkly sequins.

Check it out

Use patterned fabric instead of felt to make your decoration. Cut out the triangles with zigzag scissors to stop them from fraying. Finish off with a row of buttons down the middle.

Tip!

To sew on sequins with the beads, pull the needle through the fabric, from back to front. Thread the sequin onto the needle and then add a bead. Slide both down so they sit against the fabric. Push the needle back through the hole in the sequin and out to the back of the fabric. Add as many sequins and beads as you like in the same way!

Box clever

Store your stuff in some of these cool containers, all made from old cans and boxes!

Spongepot star-stamps!

Cut a strip of paper to fit around an empty food container and stick in place. Snip pieces of kitchen sponge into shapes. Dip the shapes into paint and print a pattern onto the container. Allow to dry.

Tip!

Look for tube-shaped containers that hold things such as potato chips or cookies. They often have lids, which are even more useful for storing your treasures safely. Just make sure to clean them out first!

Hex box

Old chocolate boxes are often an interesting shape, like this hexagon. To decorate, cut out pictures from old magazines. Spread glue over the back of each one and press down onto the box. Overlap the edges of the pictures so the box is completely covered.

On your mark, get set, splatter!

Cut a strip of paper to fit around an empty food container and stick in place. Dip a big paintbrush into some paint. Use it to flick and splatter paint all over the paper. Use different colors to create an interesting and bright splatter pattern. Allow to dry.

Tip!

This is a messy project, so spread out some old newspapers under the paper to protect the floor and table. If you can do your paint-splattering outside, that's even better!

Ladybug loot-stasher!

Cover a box with red tissue paper and carefully cut a hole in the top. Cut out a face with two spiky antennae from black cardstock. Make it a little bit bigger than the front of the box. Glue into position and stick on some eyes. Cut legs from black cardstock and glue to the bottom of the box. Decorate with black spots.

! Ask an adult for help with this craft.

Tip!

Try making your ladybug from a small tissue box that already has a hole cut in the top.

Moneybox monster

Glue colored tissue paper all the way around a tall, thin cardboard box. Cut a slot on one side to make a mouth. Stick on arms, eyes, and some colorful spots. Drop your pocket money in through the mouth and the monster will keep your savings safe. Just make sure the slot is big enough to get the money out again!

Cereal stripes

Take an empty cereal box and cut off the top. Cover the box in paper. Cut triangle shapes out of the top edge to make a zigzag pattern. Add some slick stripes to the box by sticking on strips of colored and patterned paper.

Monster mishmash

Gather up some junky scraps and let your imagination go as wild as these monsters!

You will need:

- Thick cardboard
- Pencil
- Scissors
- Bubble wrap
- Marker
- Colored cardstock
- Clear tape
- Two bottle tops
- Two buttons
- White glue

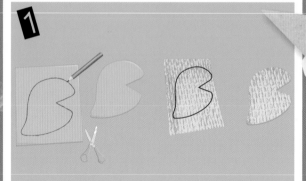

1

Draw a monster shape onto cardboard and cut out. Trace around the shape onto bubble wrap with a marker. Cut out and stick the bubble wrap to the cardboard monster.

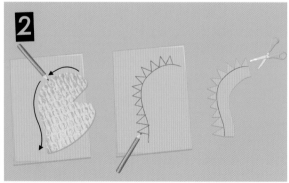

2

Place the monster down onto some more cardboard. Trace the shape of its back in pencil. Draw a zigzag, following the shape, then cut it out. Cut just below the straight pencil line so it's easier to stick in place.

3

Cut out teeth and a tongue from colored cardstock. Cut cardboard legs with clawed feet. Tape these and the zigzag strip to the back of the monster. Glue a button inside each bottle top for eyes. Glue into place.

Wild-eyed and wiggly

Make a crazy one-eyed monster! Cut out a head, body, arms, and legs from cardboard. Concertina-fold the legs. Decorate the monster with buttons and string. Add wild yarn for hair.

Tip!

Glue your finished monster onto a piece of cardboard or colored paper to make a cool picture.

Tip!

Stick the cardboard legs on at different angles so it looks like your bubble-wrap monster is walking!

Egg-o-saurus

Cut out pieces of an egg carton and glue along a monster spine to make cool humps. Stick a button on each one and add another button to make a beady eye. Draw a smile!

Grrrrrrrrrrrrrrr

221

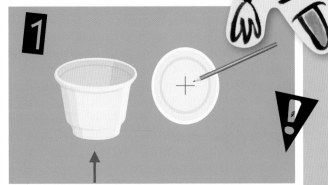

Pop-up Pals

Turn a plain yogurt cup and straw into a jolly jumping character!

You will need:

- Plastic yogurt cup
- Paint
- Tissue paper
- White glue
- Pencil
- Flexible straw
- Paintbrush
- Scissors
- Thin cardstock
- Markers
- Clear tape

⚠ Ask an adult for help with this craft.

1

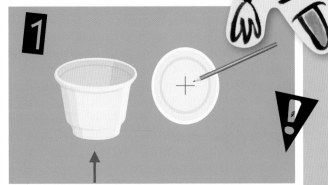

Ask an adult to make a hole in the bottom of your yogurt cup with a craft knife. Get the adult to cut two slits in a cross shape and push a pencil through to make a hole.

2

Paint your yogurt cup a bright color. You might need to brush on a few coats to cover up the words and pictures on the cup.

3

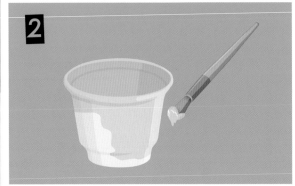

Cut out triangles of tissue paper in two or three different colors. Use white glue to stick the triangles around the edge of the pot. Do one row facing down and one facing up. Mix up the colors as you go.

4

Draw a clown onto a piece of cardstock. Color in with markers, then cut out. Tape to the straight end of your flexible straw.

5

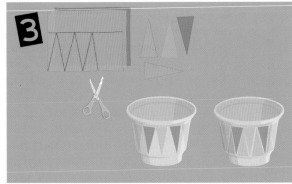

Push the straw through the hole in your yogurt cup. This is now the clown's drum! Slide the straw up and down so it looks as though the clown is jumping on the drum.

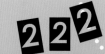

Tip!

Draw some more clowns in different jumping positions!

Tip!

Once you've pushed your straw into the yogurt cup, bend over the end so it doesn't slide out again.

Tip!

Stick a whole row of tissue triangles down before you add the next row. It's much easier to fit the shapes together this way.

Leap frog

Use your yogurt cup the right side up to turn it into a pond. Paint it blue inside and green on the outside. Decorate with grass and flowers. Add a cute frog to the end of the straw, then make him leap in and out of the pond.

Fluttering flag

Cut up your plastic bags to make this super-cool streamer flag!

You will need:

- Scissors
- Ruler
- Double-sided tape
- Plastic bags, in different colors
- Clear tape
- Garden stake

1

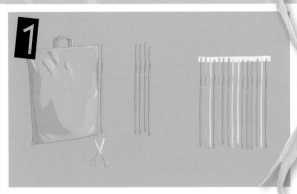

Cut strips from the long edges of your plastic bags. Cut an 8-inch strip of tape and place it down, sticky side up. Press the ends of the strips on top, leaving gaps in between. Make another strip in the same way.

2

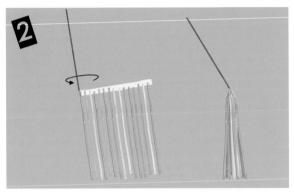

Place your garden stake over the end of the clear tape. Roll the stake along the tape so it sticks as you go. Keep going, wrapping the tape around as tightly as you can. Wrap around the second strip, too.

3

Cut a piece of plastic bag, roughly 1.5 x 2 inches. Stick double-sided tape to the back. Wrap it around the garden stake to hold the strips firmly in place.

4

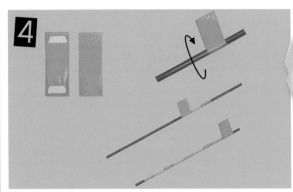

To decorate the stake, cut out a few wider strips of plastic in different colors. Add double-sided tape to the back. Wind them around the stake to make a striped pattern.

Tip!
Add some pieces of gold or silver curly ribbon on the tape strip for a cool, shimmery effect!